WHAT OTHERS SAY ABOUT THIS BOOK

"Dr. Parker's *Thoughts* exposits the unsearchable riches of Christ in Ruth, focusing on the worldwide redemptive purposes of God for all believers. This is rich commentary that will edify the saints."

-Dr. Thomas M. Strouse, MDiv,
PhD, ThD, DD, DLitt
Pastor, Bible Baptist Church,
Cromwell, Connecticut

"Having had the privilege to personally study much of the Bible under Dr. Parker, I can safely say that this new book on Ruth will be very precious to many. There is no other Bible expositor/teacher that I would recommend any more highly."

-Ralph W. Brown, Jr.
Pastor, East Side Baptist Church,
Milwaukee, Wisconsin

EXPOSITORY THOUGHTS ON
RUTH

EXPOSITORY THOUGHTS ON
RUTH

DR. CHARLES L. PARKER

TATE PUBLISHING
AND ENTERPRISES, LLC

Expository Thoughts on Ruth
Copyright © 2011 by Dr. Charles L. Parker. All rights reserved.

No part of this publication may be reproduced, stored in a retrieval system or transmitted in any way by any means, electronic, mechanical, photocopy, recording or otherwise without the prior permission of the author except as provided by USA copyright law.

Scripture quotations are taken from the *Holy Bible, King James Version* ©, Cambridge, 1769. Used by permission. All rights reserved.

This book is designed to provide accurate and authoritative information with regard to the subject matter covered. This information is given with the understanding that neither the author nor Tate Publishing, LLC is engaged in rendering legal, professional advice. Since the details of your situation are fact dependent, you should additionally seek the services of a competent professional.

The opinions expressed by the author are not necessarily those of Tate Publishing, LLC.

Published by Tate Publishing & Enterprises, LLC
127 E. Trade Center Terrace | Mustang, Oklahoma 73064 USA
1.888.361.9473 | www.tatepublishing.com

Tate Publishing is committed to excellence in the publishing industry. The company reflects the philosophy established by the founders, based on Psalm 68:11,
"The Lord gave the word and great was the company of those who published it."

Book design copyright © 2011 by Tate Publishing, LLC. All rights reserved.
Cover design by Joel Uber
Interior design by Chelsea Womble

Published in the United States of America

ISBN: 978-1-61346-704-6
1. Religion, Biblical Commentary, Old Testament
2. Religion, Christian Life, Devotional
11.09.20

This book is dedicated to my wife, Bonnie. She has faithfully encouraged and strengthened me in the Lord for many years and is a wonderful mother to all our children and grandmother to all our grandchildren. In a very real sense, our relationship is a reverse of what is found in Ruth in that she found me in a "far country" and was instrumental in me coming to the Lord.

PREFACE

The basic format of this book is simple. The entire book of Ruth has been divided into daily devotional readings. At the beginning of each day's reading the Scripture verses under consideration will be written out. Following the verses will be comments on those verses. Thus, by taking each day as a separate reading, the reader may progress through the book of Ruth with specific applications of the biblical truths in the passages for each day.

The purpose of this study is to encourage each reader to take the message of Ruth personally and enter into all the will of God day by day. In order to fulfill this purpose, at the end of each week's devotional readings the reader will encounter questions designed to make the application of the devotional studies personal. If the study were to be followed exactly as presented, it would take seven weeks. Of course, each reader is welcome to use the material in whatever manner is best for him or her. May the Lord bless the endeavor for all who participate!

I recommend that the readings be done on a weekly basis, Monday through Friday, leaving Saturday and Sunday for meditation and local church involvement.

INTRODUCTION

This is a very precious book revealing, as it does, so much of the staggering wonder of the redemptive will of God for His people. As we move along through the pages of this divine revelation, short as it is, we will encounter what might be the most stunning Old Testament revelation of the fact that the redemptive love of God in Jesus Christ brings the believing child of God into the center of all the will of God. We shall also come to see that this redemptive love of God crosses all barriers and is operative even in the very darkest of hours. His blessed redemptive love reaches all the way out into despised Moab to bring a humble, undeserving, yet believing Moabitess to Himself at Bethlehem and farther still into the very lineage of the Son of God. This same divine purpose is fulfilled in the present day as well when His redemptive love finds every child of God, however far from Him he might be, bringing that trembling believer into the center of His great, Christ-glorifying purpose for that life.

GENERAL IMPRESSIONS OF THE BOOK OF RUTH

We will begin with four general impressions of this marvelous book, using an acrostic on the word Ruth.

REDEMPTIVE REALITY

This precious book helps keep our focus where it belongs when we study the Bible. It comes between two other books in the Bible in which there is great turmoil. In Judges, we see the terrible reality of how things deteriorate when men's lives are characterized by doing that which is right in their own eyes. There will be conflict and rampant unbelief. The enemy will have open doors through which to work and bring about confusion and strife.

Then, in First Samuel, we see how far astray men go when such conditions prevail. Men have no desire to submit to the rule of God, and they follow the leadership of men, moving further and further into darkness and despair. Their leaders have no light in them and find themselves turning to the lord of darkness for "light." So it was with Saul, and so it is with all men who reject the light of truth as it is in God's King.

Right in the midst of such days, we are prone to have our focus turned aside from all the will of God. It is so easy to lose sight of all that the Lord is still doing because it is so obscured by the noise and the bright lights so commonly prevailing when men are exalting one another. When man is exalted, God is dethroned and darkness and conflict predominate. But lest the righteous despair, the Lord includes this wonderful book of Ruth. It is intended to encourage us to keep our eyes upon the ongoing redemptive work of God.

To put it clearly, in Ruth, we are shown that even in the midst of very discouraging days, God will go all the way to despised Moab to capture and captivate the heart of a young girl. He will bring her back to Bethlehem (the house of bread) and, through His eternal redemptive purposes in Christ, bring her into the line of royalty. God had His eye upon this Moabite girl before the foundation of the world, intending to call forth out of her loins the one who would become the great Kinsman-Redeemer of all mankind, the King of kings and Lord of lords.

This blessed book will have the effect of undergirding our hearts when they begin to waver due to our dwelling among men who exalt themselves among themselves and seek to shut out God entirely. No matter how things are outwardly among men, our God is pressing on in the completion of His worldwide redemptive purposes in Christ. And each one of us is offered the privilege of taking his or her own place in all the redemptive will of God for his own life.

How precious this truly is. When everything is unsatisfying and seemingly meaningless all around us, we may take heart. God is on the throne whether men like it or not. He is working behind the scenes to bring about His redemptive purposes in Christ. And my life does have deep and precious meaning as I align myself by faith with His redemptive will for me. As Paul later says, I might very well be steadfast, unmovable, always abounding in the work of the Lord forasmuch as I know that my labor is not in vain in the Lord (1 Corinthians 15:58).

UNIFIED HISTORY

As we study this tremendous book, we are struck with the one key truth that so clearly unifies all of Old Testament history. This is no small matter since many of God's people today struggle to see the connection of the history of Israel with themselves in the present day. A common question among many Christians when confronted with the Old Testament passages related to the nation of Israel is, *What does that have to do with me?*

The book of Ruth helps dispel such uncertainty and replace it with strong confidence in the unified connectedness of the redemptive will of God throughout all stages of human history. In the first verse, we are told the present setting of the events in the book. We are told that these events transpired in the days when the judges ruled. That ties it to the present tense in Ruth's day. But it also serves to link it to our day in a very real sense because we are certainly living in days when men do that which is right in their own eyes, paying little attention to the redemptive will of God for their lives.

But it is interesting to note toward the end of this short book that the folks there in Bethlehem in Ruth's day had no difficulty linking what was happening among them to historical events of at least four hundred years in the past. This they do when they refer to the days of Rachel and Leah (4:11) and Pharez and Tamar (4:12). These Bethlehemites clearly understood the connection between what was happening among them in their own day and what the Lord had been doing among their forefathers. God's people in the early twenty-first century need to have similar faith. What the Lord is seeking to do among us today is directly linked to all that he has been doing in the fulfillment of His worldwide, redemptive purposes throughout human history. A consciousness of this reality has the power to literally transform the lives of Christians today who often feel that what is happening in their personal lives doesn't make any real difference.

All throughout human history, there has been really only one leading reality underlying all human events, whether small or great. It is the great conflict of the seeds identified in Genesis 3:15. Even among the people of God in Old Testament days and when all men were doing whatever pleased themselves, there was a believing remnant who saw the connection between their personal lives and the grand divine plan. We, like them, have been brought into the line of the seed of the woman. What God is doing in each one of our lives has great significance.

When the Lord connected with Ruth in Moab, she had not previously been conscious of any grand scheme of things. She had certainly seen glimmerings of truth, evident in the life of her mother-in-law. But she had never dreamed that she, herself, could ever hope to take such a significant place in God's worldwide plans. Nevertheless, she was brought from obscurity and wretchedness directly into the line of the great King Himself. The book closes out with the amazing lineage from Pharez through King David. And the entire line is full of staggering wonder. Pharez was the son of Judah with Tamar, an illicit birth. Salmon begat Boaz, yes, but of Rahab, the former Canaanite harlot. And now, Boaz begets Obed of Ruth, the despised Moabitess.

Clearly, the one thing that unifies all that God has been doing throughout all ages of human history is His grace. It is the one thing that His enemies never seem to grasp. It is the most powerful reality of all. And we must not ever underestimate it, for to do so is to fail to truly know Him for who He is.

TRUE REIGNING

It bears mentioning again that the position of the book of Ruth is significant. As we have seen, it is preceded by the book of Judges, characterized by utter turmoil as men live according to their own counsels. The entire period of Israel's history reveals the drift away from God-sufficiency that had so characterized the times of Joshua's leadership. As men move further away from being ruled by the Lord and His purposes for their lives, a repeating cycle develops among them. They struggle with purpose and direction, choose their own way, and find themselves under the rule of Gentile warlords and kings. They cry out to their God, who hears them and graciously sends them a deliverer, and they are freed from their bondage. But their freedom is short-lived because they use it to go their own way again, and the cycle renews.

Ruth is followed by the book of First Samuel. In this book, together with its companion book, Second Samuel, it is revealed that Israel has now come to the place of clearly rejecting God's rule over them. This is specifically stated by the Lord Himself in First Samuel 8:7: "They have rejected me, that I should not reign over them." Israel clamors for a king and is given Saul and later David. While one is a man after their own hearts and the other is a man after God's own heart, neither of them is God; neither of them is the true King. These two books (First and Second Samuel) portray the terrible reality of a people who think of themselves as the "people of God" but who sit on the thrones of their own lives. All throughout them, the Lord is reoffering Himself to Israel as their King.

Sandwiched between Judges and the books of Samuel is this marvelous book of Ruth. One of the best ways to truly grasp the impact of this perfectly placed book is to understand its relationship to these others. During the days when Israel was drifting away from God's leadership among them, when men chose instead to rule their own lives, God was still on the throne working out His wonderful redemptive purposes. When all those around them in Israel were in turmoil, seeking their own way, there were some who sought the Lord and delighted in

His reign in their lives. The lives of Boaz and Ruth, as pictured in this book, are the very expression of what the Apostle Paul later writes in Romans 5:17, when he speaks of men who "shall reign in life by…Jesus Christ." While all around them are busily establishing their own thrones in life, Boaz and Ruth (among others) are busily surrendering theirs.

What an amazing revelation. Men can be ruled by the Lord. And their lives can have that fragrance of genuine reigning in life. The book of Ruth reminds us to sustain a consciousness of the believing remnant all throughout Scripture. Yes, men might and will reject the reign of God, rejecting His redemptive purposes for their lives, but there will always be a believing remnant among the multitudes of religious ones.

Ruth is the Lord's great invitation to all of us to descend to the throne by surrendering the rule of our lives to Him. No matter how the multitudes around us behave themselves, even the religious crowd, we may delight in a life lived entirely for His purposes. In Ruth, we see once and for all the staggering difference it makes when men and women say a wholehearted, "Yes," to His glory and His redemptive plan for their lives. It affects everything and everyone.

HUMAN FRAILTY

All that we have been saying about the book of Ruth is only rightly understood when seen in the light of the overwhelming human frailty that is so evident on every level in the "story."

First of all, there is the clear revelation of human frailty identified in the very first verse. "Now it came to pass in the days when the judges ruled, that there was a famine in the land. And a certain man of Bethlehem-Judah went to sojourn in the country of Moab, he, and his wife, and his two sons." Men are enormously affected by the events that transpire in their environments. Here, we find the family of a certain man of Bethlehem-Judah reacting to a famine in his native land. The man is clearly the leader of his family and decides to move his family away from all that had been home to them because of the severe effects of the famine. We will see more of this in the full study of the book later. But it is clear that the Lord ultimately uses this man's frailty to accomplish divine purposes.

In this same verse, we encounter the mention of the country Moab. This calls to mind the tragic events in the lives of other frail human beings long before the days of Elimelech. Lot and his family fled the judgment rained down from heaven upon Sodom and Gomorrah. Lot's wife looked back and was turned into a pillar of salt. Lot's two daughters eventually had illicit relationships with their own father and bore children. Moab was one of these illegitimate sons. Ultimately, God placed a curse upon the descendants of Moab, forbidding Israel to have anything to do with them.

By the fifth verse of this first chapter of Ruth, we are immersed in human frailty in even greater terms. In this short space, we are told that while in Moab the man and both of his sons have died, leaving his wife and his son's wives to grapple with life without husbands. It is easy to see how overwhelming our own frailty may be. We all find ourselves confronted with our own helplessness repeatedly all throughout life.

But this is not all, for Naomi, Elimelech's widowed wife, is now utterly disgraced. She obediently followed her husband into a far country years ago, under very stressful circumstances. Her sons have matured, taken wives of the Moabites, and then died. As though the death of her own husband had not been enough, now she longs to return to her own people; but if she goes back, she must do so in disgrace, having sojourned so long among those who dwelt under the curse of God. What will her old friends say? How will she be treated?

Even more, one of her daughters-in-law, Ruth, is determined to make the return trip with Naomi. Human frailty will manifest itself again as many will "talk behind their hands" as they look and point and gossip. "Have you ever seen such a thing? There is poor old Naomi, coming home, but to what? Who will redeem her husband's land and inheritance? And who is that girl with her? Is that one of those Moabite women? Oh my!" How often our frailty hinders the revelation of God in us! How unlike Him we so often behave ourselves.

There is so much more of human frailty in this startling book. Yet, the blessed thing we must see is not only the human weakness but the divine strength that so fully overcomes it. As the book closes, there is the revelation of the birth of a frail, little baby boy. His name is Obed, and he is the son of Boaz and Ruth. But as we follow the remaining details of his lineage as they are given at the end of the book, we are reminded of the birth of another baby boy in all his frailty many years later: David, the one who would sit upon the throne of all Israel. And does this not cause our hearts to leap as we contemplate the amazing reality of the yet greater birth to come? For David prefigures the greater Son of David, the Lord, Jesus Christ. Though born into human frailty and nurtured at a human woman's breast, this one would grapple with the very devil himself, defeating him and winning heaven for many frail sons and daughters of Adam in the bargain.

It behooves us to enter into the staggering statement made by one of the Lamb's apostles, the Apostle Paul, many years after Ruth, when he said, "Therefore I take pleasure in infirmities, in reproaches, in necessities, in persecutions, in distresses for Christ's sake: for when I am weak, then am I strong" (2 Corinthians 12:10). To the degree that the full message of Ruth genuinely sinks into our souls we shall also have the faith to know that our human frailty is the very platform upon which the Lord delights in making His power known.

Having acquired a general sense of the message of this wonderful book, we now turn our attention to the daily readings.

WEEK ONE

RUTH 1:1-2

Now it came to pass in the days when the judges
ruled, that there was a famine in the land. And a
certain man of Bethlehem-Judah went to sojourn
in the country of Moab, he, and his wife, and his
two sons. And the name of the man was Elimelech,
and the name of his wife Naomi, and the name of
his two sons Mahlon and Chilion, Ephrathites of
Bethlehem-Judah. And they came into the country
of Moab, and continued there.

As we have seen, the events in Ruth coincide with the
days of the judges when men "did that which was right
in their own eyes." To the American ear, this might
sound like something to be desired, but that is certainly
not how the Holy Spirit means it. When all men do that
which is right in their own eyes, the result is the roller-
coaster ride described so eloquently in Judges. Few men
deem it "right" to surrender their lives to be lived for the
glory of God or for His redemptive purposes.

It was during such a period of time that the Lord
sent a famine into the land of His own people. This particular family actually lived right in the Bethlehem area,

the very area where David the king would ultimately be born and grow to manhood. The name Bethlehem means "house of bread." There is certainly irony in the fact that the Lord sent the famine among those dwelling in the house of bread. God is sovereign in His disposition of things in the lives of all men. There is a special kind of blessedness that attaches to this fact as He works in the lives of His own people though. Therefore, we are right to be expectant when He deems it appropriate to bring trials into the lives of His children. The Lord had His redemptive purposes in mind when He allowed conditions among His own people to deteriorate to the point of outright famine in the land. This fact forms the very substance of the heartbeat of this book of Ruth.

We are told the names of the family members who accompanied Elimelech away from Bethlehem. Their Hebrew meanings are instructive. Elimelech means "my God is King," a fact that underlies the entire record of events in the book. Naomi means "sweetness" or "graciousness," a name that literally conveys the leading element of her personal character. Mahlon means "weakly" and suggests the nature of Elimelech's faith, which seduced him to flee the famine by going away from the house of bread into an ungodly land. Finally, Chilion means "pining" or "wasting." This young man's name certainly suggests that which awaited them in that alien land, though they could not have known it ahead of time.

We are also told the name of the land to which they fled in their weak faith. It was Moab. The relationship between Israel and Moab is not a good one. The previous scriptural record identifies that the Lord Himself forbade Israel to associate with the Moabites, even to the point of disallowing Moabites in their congregation at all (Deuteronomy 23:3).

So then, what we have before us in these two verses is the record of facts. The Lord sends a famine among His people, certainly to try them as they lived their lives out according to their own choices and decisions. This man and his family leave the "house of bread" and flee to a despised country, one which the Lord forbade them to mingle with in any sense.

What will be the outcome? Can we expect anything good to come of it? And why is this little book sandwiched between Judges and 1 Samuel? What are we to learn from what the Lord records for us here? May the Lord truly help us to receive what He has for us as we continue.

RUTH 1:3–5

And Elimelech Naomi's husband died; and she was left, and her two sons. And they took them wives of the women of Moab; the name of the one was Orpah, and the name of the other Ruth: and they dwelled there about ten years. And Mahlon and Chilion died also both of them; and the woman was left of her two sons and her husband.

In today's passage, we encounter yet further trials laid upon the hearts of Naomi and her daughters-in-law. There is no controversy that the greater weight of the burden fell upon Naomi. She is far from friends and family in a land that lies under the curse of God. She has come here by way of being a submissive and obedient wife, following her husband as he led them in unbelief away from the land of promise into a country that God calls His "wash pot" (Psalm 60:8 and 108:9) Now her husband has died, followed in death within ten years by his sons.

We do well to recall the meaning of the names of Naomi's husband, together with the names of his sons. God has His own purposes for the lives of His people. Sometimes their purposes for their lives differ greatly from His, a sad fact that characterizes many who claim to be God's people throughout all dispensations. When men move in unbelief away from all the will of God for their lives and sustain that direction in spite of all that God does to turn them, they will invariably find themselves pining or wasting.

But God is still the King. When the lives of the very people whom God has chosen to bear His image among the fallen sons of Adam become filled with weakness and pining, God might very well end those lives. The Lord, Jesus Christ Himself told us as much when He said, "Every branch in me that beareth not fruit he [God] taketh away" (John 15:2). Few Christians would select this as their life verse or even as a favorite passage. Yet its truth remains. When men's lives become unfruitful in the fulfillment of God's wonderful redemptive purposes, they become forfeit.

It is stunning, isn't it, how much difference ten years can make? Ten years earlier Naomi was at home in Bethlehem, among friends and family, with two maturing young sons. In the intervening years, she has dealt with famine, her husband's failing faith, and being uprooted and moving away from family and friends to a land she knew to be apart from the favor of God. She has watched her husband die there. Her heart has been tried as her sons have taken wives from among the Moabite girls. Mothers always ache when their sons step outside the path of God's apparent blessing in their marriages. Now, the boys have also died. She is left a childless widow with two young women linked to her through her sons but plainly unlikely to be welcome among her own people. Yes, ten years can make a staggering difference.

Most who read the record of these events in the beginning of this book can testify to the same reality. As we come to this place in the divine narrative, we are distressed for Naomi's sake, knowing something of her heartache and despair. Hopefully, however, for many of us, there is that sense of something moving beneath it all, really Someone. Throughout all the decades of our own experience, since we have come to know Him, this awareness of His personal involvement in all the events of our lives has perhaps sustained us even in times so trying we scarcely believed we could navigate our way through them at all.

We await the further divine record with anticipation, knowing that the weeping might endure for a night but that somehow, miraculously if necessary, joy will come in the morning. As we mature in our own faith, we literally come to expect this of our God. He is like that.

RUTH 1:6–7

Then she arose with her daughters in law, that she might return from the country of Moab: for she had heard in the country of Moab how that the LORD had visited his people in giving them bread. Wherefore she went forth out of the place where she

was, and her two daughters in law with her; and they
went on the way to return unto the land of Judah.

Today's passage brings us to a key point in the narrative.
There is more here than meets the eye at first glance.
May the Lord help us to be attentive to all that He is
putting before us in these two blessed verses.

Naomi submissively followed her husband away
from all that she held dear. They came to dwell in an
alien land, among a despised people. It was a famine
that drove them there. But in a very real sense, Naomi
has encountered a far greater famine of sorts in Moab.
In the same way that circumstances have brought them
there, it will be circumstances that bring Naomi to the
point of going home. What reason would she now have
for staying in Moab? Years ago, as they had fled east-
ward, everything to the west seemed bleak and gloomy.
Now all that had filled her sky with any sunshine in
Moab was gone. There was a pall hanging over the
land for Naomi, with her only connection now being
through her daughters-in-law. But looking westward
now brought hope and a small measure of expectation.
She heard that the Lord had once again blessed His
people with plenty of food.

It is only natural that her heart would already be
yearning in measure for all that remained in Bethlehem.
At least there she would once again be among her own
people. In times of great heartache, we all long for some
place of understanding if not outright comfort. This we
expect to find among our own people.

It is instructive to consider how much the Lord uses
our natural heart inclinations to ultimately bring about
His purposes in our lives. Certainly He knew the heart

of Elimelech years ago, when the original famine swept through the land of Judah. God was not at all surprised when Elimelech reacted in unbelief, choosing to go away into Moab rather than seeking help from a kinsman in the land of promise. In fact, as the events in this book move across the written page, we see very clearly just how much the Lord used Elimelech's unbelief to accomplish things that would have been left undone otherwise.

But we find the same thing to be true now that Naomi is bereft of all her family and, with them, all her hope for a name among her own people. The Lord knew very well that Naomi's heart was in agony in Moab, that she felt terribly misplaced and abandoned there. So it was that He saw to it that she received word that things were better in Bethlehem. His timing in all things is perfect.

She sets out with her two daughters-in-law to return to Bethlehem. Her girls are surely nervous and apprehensive, yet they determine to do the right thing, remaining linked to the vestiges of the family into which they had married. This speaks highly of their character. But it also speaks highly of Naomi. She evidently had a strong influence on both of them. It is here that we begin to realize that Naomi's spiritual stature was more advanced than that of her husband. One wonders, had he been yet alive, if there would have been any inclination to return home. We have the distinct impression that great things lie just across the horizon for Naomi. May we have such anticipation when we are as bereft as Naomi was at this point.

RUTH 1:8-10

And Naomi said unto her two daughters in law, "Go, return each to her mother's house: the LORD deal kindly with you, as ye have dealt with the dead, and with me. The LORD grant you that ye may find rest, each of you in the house of her husband." Then she kissed them; and they lifted up their voice, and wept. And they said unto her, "Surely we will return with thee unto thy people."

Naomi now begins to release her daughters-in-law from any obligation they might feel to her personally. She realizes that for them to remain with her as she returns to Bethlehem would mean that they must literally leave all and attempt to forge an entirely new life among a people that have historically shunned all Moabites. It would be asking a great deal of them, something Naomi herself has no right to ask. God alone may make such demands of anyone.

She is quick to point out to them that they still have their lives before them and that perhaps their wisest course of action may lie in going home to their own mothers and seeing if the Lord will provide them with husbands yet again in their own homeland. She manifests genuine wisdom and even compassion, though she herself feels utterly forsaken and alone.

There is a remarkable detail often overlooked in this entire passage, in verses six through thirteen, as Naomi exhorts her daughters-in-law. Though she is in anguish in her own heart, Naomi mentions the blessed name of the LORD no less than four times as she seeks to comfort and strengthen them. This title for the Lord, using all capital letters, refers to the Hebrew name Jehovah.

It is the name the Lord uses for Himself when revealing Himself in covenant relationship with the children of Israel. It speaks of His faithfulness and unchanging commitment to His redemptive purposes through them.

The significance of Naomi using this specific title for the Lord is that even in her deepest trial, she clearly has a sense of His unwavering involvement in her life and the lives of all others as well. She speaks of His faithfulness in visiting His people with bread again (verse six). Then she commends Him unto her daughters-in-law as the Lord who they may expect to deal kindly with them and to provide them with new husbands (verses eight through nine). Yet, when she refers to herself, she is clearly smitten with the fact that the Lord's hand has gone out against her (verse 13).

Were she able to read her own story, as we are, she might well skip a few pages farther along to find that His hand is most definitely *not* gone out against her. But that lies in the future for her at this point. We do well not to criticize her too harshly for not being able to grasp all that the Lord is doing through her deep trial. It is, after all, so familiar in our own lives. We are apt to measure what the Lord is doing by the way the experience feels to us at the moment. Yet, all the while, He is at work bringing about greater things than we could have dared to hope for.

We are specifically told that these things were written for our edification (Romans 15:4, 1 Corinthians 10:11). In other words, when the Lord worked His redemptive purposes out in the lives of these Old Testament saints, He intended that the scriptural record of their maturing faith should become a means of deepening our faith as well. We are left to contemplate how much the Lord may use our trials of faith as a means of strengthening the faith of others.

RUTH 1:11–13

And Naomi said, "Turn again, my daughters: why will ye go with me? are there yet any more sons in my womb, that they may be your husbands? Turn again, my daughters, go your way; for I am too old to have an husband. If I should say, I have hope, if I should have an husband also to night, and should also bear sons; Would ye tarry for them till they were grown? would ye stay for them from having husbands? nay, my daughters; for it grieveth me much for your sakes that the hand of the LORD is gone out against me."

The quality of these girls is clearly revealed as they both (verse ten) identify their intention to return to Palestine with her. But Naomi quickly admonishes them to think about their decision again. She reminds them that she has little to offer them. She is too old to have children again. Even if she could have children, would it make any sense that they could consider waiting for them to grow to manhood so that they could marry them? Even in this it seems to Naomi that the hand of the Lord has gone out against her.

Perhaps now is the time to introduce the key truth that the Lord seems to be placing before us in the first chapter of this marvelous book. We have already suggested that the thrust of the book as a whole is that God, in His redemptive love, is at work through all things in our lives to bring every believing child of God into the center of all the will of God. The specific way this central message is carried forward in chapter one might be well embodied in the statement, "The redeeming love of God is *Winnowing Love.*" The pathway for Naomi (and, as we shall see, Ruth) from the wash pot of God (Moab) into the very lineage of the King begins with very strong winnowing. It is so for each one of us as well, though we would rather it not be so. If we are to be brought from the far country into the fullness of God's redemptive purposes for our lives, it might at first, or at any point along the way, require the Lord to bring us through a powerful winnowing process. *yes!*

According to the dictionary, winnowing is a process of separating the good from the bad. It is most often related to the harvesting of grain. The stalks of grain are cut in the field and gathered into sheaves or bundles. Those bundles are then brought to the threshing floor where the winnowing begins. They are beaten against the ground to loosen the heads of grain as much as possible. During this process, the threshing floor becomes covered with both grain and chaff (pieces of the stalks that have been broken off and are laying among the grain). Any stalks that still retain heads of grain on them are cut off short, near the head, and allowed to fall to the floor as well. This mixture of grain and chaff is then gathered into piles and lain in batches into a shallow winnowing basket that has holes in it large enough to allow the grain alone to fall through but small enough to restrain the chaff. The mixture is then repeatedly cast into the air, allowing the wind to carry away as much chaff as possible, while the heavier heads of grain fall through and are gathered on the floor. It is through this process that the useless chaff is separated (winnowed) from the desired fruit of the harvest.

This is clearly a most traumatic process for the grain to endure. Yet, it is absolutely necessary. Apart from this process or one similar to it carried out in the present day by machinery, the fruit of the harvest would never be made available to make bread or cereal or become in any way useful for the furtherance of life.

So it is with God's winnowing love. It is because He loves us so much that he will winnow us so that we become fruitful. Unless we are willing to be thoroughly winnowed, we cannot be fruitful. His wonderful redemptive purposes in our lives will never be realized. It is even as our Lord later said, "Except a grain of wheat fall into the earth and die, it abideth alone." John 12:24.

QUESTIONS FOR FURTHER CONSIDERATION ON RUTH 1:1–13

[1] To what extent, do you think, does America in the twenty-first century correspond to the times when the Judges ruled, and men did that which was right in their own eyes?

[2] To the degree that the correspondence is strong, what effect ought this to have on our faith in God fulfilling His purposes in our lives?

[3] Can you recognize what the Lord has done in your life that was a matter of His winnowing love? What are some of the details? Looking back on them now in the light of God's winnowing love for Naomi and Ruth, is it easier for you to thank Him for His faithfulness?

[4] Do you think the winnowing process is always the same for each of God's saints? If not, why not?

 [5] Have you paused to reflect upon the goodness of the Lord in reaching out to you when you were in "Moab"? Can you worship Him for exchanging your "Moab life" for your part in His worldwide redemptive purposes?

WEEK TWO

RUTH 1:14-15

And they lifted up their voice, and wept again: and Orpah kissed her mother in law; but Ruth clave unto her. And she said, "Behold, thy sister in law is gone back unto her people, and unto her gods: return thou after thy sister in law."

Today's passage plainly identifies the real issues underlying the Lord's redemptive purposes in this wonderful book. Naomi is going to go back home to Bethlehem, where the Lord is blessing His people with plenty of bread again. She has exhorted her daughters-in-law to go back to their own families with the hope that by remaining in their homeland, they may once again find husbands, something they had little expectation of were they to go to Bethlehem with her.

Now we see that Orpah takes Naomi's advice. She kisses Naomi and returns home to her family. But Naomi, speaking to Ruth once again, emphasizes that Orpah has not only returned unto her people but also unto her gods. This is the real heart of the entire matter. It shows how both Orpah and Ruth, through their association with Naomi and her family, had been exposed to truth concerning the God of Israel. Marrying into that family brought them into contact with Him, and it was now something about which they were confronted with a clear-cut choice. If they went back to their own people, they were choosing also to go back to their own gods, forsaking all that they had come to know about the God of Naomi.

This simple parting of the ways between Naomi and her daughter-in-law, Orpah, was far more consequential than it may appear to the casual reader of Scripture. Apparently, the knowledge of Naomi's God was not enough to compel her to make the choice to leave her family behind. Perhaps it was only "head knowledge," as we are prone to say in our own day. It might well be that the Lord was not real enough to Orpah to necessitate her separation from the religion she had grown up with over the years. What is clear is that, for whatever reason, Orpah went back to her own people and to her own gods and the true and living God was forsaken in the bargain.

But this leaves us standing in the middle of the road, as it were, with Naomi and her other daughter-in-law, Ruth. What will Ruth decide to do? Naomi gives her, once again, the same opportunity she had given Orpah. Ruth can also go back to her people and to her gods. She is to make no mistake about it; going back to her people will be going back to her gods as well. For centuries, the Moabites have not wanted to have anything to do with the God of Israel. When Israel came up out of Egyptian bondage, Moab was one of the nations that set themselves against Israel and against her God. Moab had made it clear that she wanted nothing to do with the fulfillment of the eternal redemptive purposes of God in Jesus Christ.

It might be that there will be someone reading these words who is likewise standing in the middle of the road, unclear about which way to go. It would be natural and easy simply to align with your own people, turning away from any serious commitment to the eternal redemptive purposes of God in Jesus Christ like Orpah did. It might not even mean turning away from being a Christian. Many who attend genuine Christian churches keep themselves aloof from personally entering into the call of God on their lives to live entirely for His redemptive purposes in Christ. Standing in the middle of the road, undecided, might be the leading characteristic of Christianity in the modern era. For Ruth, at least, the choice was a very clear one, as we shall see momentarily. She understood that going one way meant going on with Naomi's God and that going back meant forsaking Him for other gods.

RUTH 1:16–17

And Ruth said, "Entreat me not to leave thee, or to return from following after thee: for whither thou goest, I will go; and where thou lodgest, I will lodge: thy people shall be my people, and thy God my God: Where thou diest, will I die, and there will I be buried: the LORD do so to me, and more also, if ought but death part thee and me."

In these two verses, we encounter the budding faith of this Moabite girl, Ruth. Naomi had told Ruth that Orpah had decided to return to her people and to her gods. Lest any should think that we have made more of this choice than is appropriate, we find in Ruth's response to Naomi

in today's passage clear evidence that she plainly understood what the choices were with which she was faced.
In these two short verses, Ruth's life is openly committed
to an entirely new path and purpose.

Naomi suggested that Ruth might want to follow
the same path chosen by Orpah. In her response, Ruth
mentions no less than six clear aspects of her own commitment. She says that she will remain linked to Naomi,
though it demand of her that she: go wherever Naomi
goes, live wherever Naomi lives, become one with
Naomi's people, worship Naomi's God, die alongside
Naomi, and be buried together with Naomi. What Ruth
is saying is very clear. She has entirely cast in her lot with
Naomi, regardless of the outcome.

We must ask ourselves, "What would compel a
young woman from a foreign country to do such a
thing?" But before considering any possible answers to
such a question, we must remember a few other details.
Naomi would be returning to a land in which Moabites
were not welcome under any circumstances. Also, Naomi
would be returning to a very uncertain future. The property previously owned by her husband would return to
his own family, and it would be up to them to determine what would happen with Naomi. Naomi had cast
in her lot with her husband many years previously, and
he, along with her two sons, had died in Moab. She had
no personal prospects at all in her homeland. Thus, she
had no way of offering any kind of living or care to her
daughter-in-law, Ruth. Naomi was returning to a culture
that pronounced blessings upon women who bore male
children but looked askance at those who had no sons as
heirs in their families. And Ruth would certainly have

very dim hopes of marrying any serious Israelite man since she was a Moabitess.

Now, once again we may ask our question, "What would compel a young woman, under such severe circumstances, to entirely throw in her lot with her mother-in-law?" The hint we need is brought out in the seventeenth verse, where we find Ruth exclaiming, "The LORD do so to me, and more also, if ought but death part thee and me." Evidently, Ruth has in some way come to the beginnings of a personal relationship with the God of Naomi. As we proceed through our considerations of this blessed book, we will have ample opportunity to see the faith of Naomi. For the present, we may simply say that the primary way Ruth would have encountered the God of Israel would have been either through her own husband, Mahlon, or his family. But Elimelech seemed to have little faith, fleeing his own homeland under stress and taking his family to Moab, as we have seen. And if Ruth's budding faith was primarily related to her husband, one might expect that she would have little reason to press on after his death. And Ruth said plainly to Naomi, "*Your* God shall be my God." So then, it would seem that Naomi's faith and willingness to entrust herself entirely to the God of Israel had a very powerful impact upon Ruth. May it be that our faith, even in great trial, will thus impact others to trust Him.

RUTH 1:18–19

When she saw that she was stedfastly minded to go with her, then she left speaking unto her. So they two went until they came to Bethlehem. And it

came to pass, when they were come to Bethlehem,
that all the city was moved about them, and they
said, "Is this Naomi?"

In spite of all of Naomi's exhortations to Ruth to return
to her own people and to her own gods, Ruth is determined to accompany her back to Bethlehem. We have
seen already that this certainly speaks of the element of
budding faith that is discernible in Ruth's life. In our first
verse today, we find that Naomi finally stopped trying to
talk Ruth out of her intention to go with her. This suggests a significant aspect of true faith even in its earliest
moments of development in the heart of a true believer.
If that faith is genuinely based upon God's revelation of
Himself in His Word, which we shall see is clearly the
case with both Naomi and Ruth, then it simply cannot
be shaken. You might just as well tell such a person that
her faith will bring her to impassable rivers and unscal-
able mountains. You might even suggest that her faith
will bring her against unconquerable enemies by the
dozens, hindering her passage with ferocity henceforth
unimaginable. No such considerations will move her.
She has seen Him with the eyes of faith, and nothing
can trouble her again.

The question arises for each reader of these words:
Have we thus seen Him with the eyes of faith? Are we
too easily swayed in our determination to go into all the
will of God? We read of the Lord's own words later as
He tells His disciples that to go on with Him in faith
will mean leaving family and holdings, yea everything,
but that the ultimate rewards will make such "sacri-
fices" seem relatively insignificant (Matthew 19:29). This
young Moabite girl made exactly this kind of decision

centuries before the Lord came in human flesh among us. Why should such a thing seem so unusual among those who claim to be His genuine followers today?

In our second verse for today, we get our first glimpse at the responses awaiting Naomi as she and Ruth begin to reenter Bethlehem. It is as we had thought in our earlier contemplations. There are those who are already beginning the unending chain of gossip that becomes like a series of daggers plunged into the very heart of the already aching one. It begins innocently enough. Someone simply asks, "Is this actually Naomi, the wife of Elimelech?" It has, after all, been a very long time since anyone has seen her in Bethlehem. And surely word has reached her homeland about the tragic deaths of her husband and her two sons, the latter cut off in the prime of early-married life.

But how often does conjectural and speculative gossip stop at its first intersection? Everyone would soon be fully aware of the fact that though her men folk all died in Moab, some Moabite girl was with her now. And isn't it a terrible burden for her to have to bear that she had ever been in Moab in the first place? Consider the shame she must feel every day! And now she is burdened also with having to tend to this Moabite girl. Why, that girl must be very brash to demand that her mother-in-law now take care of her! Seeing Naomi without a husband, having little expectation of honor and respect, now certainly ought to make each one of these faithful Bethlehemites pleased with themselves, that they, at least, had not made such bad decisions in days gone by.

It will certainly take some kind of a miracle to restore Naomi's place of respect among her own people as she moves into her aged years. This prepares us with the right kind of heart expectation as we continue to learn more about the wonderful redemptive grace of God.

RUTH 1:20–21

And she said unto them, "Call me not Naomi, call me Mara: for the Almighty hath dealt very bitterly with me. I went out full and the LORD hath brought me home again empty: why then call ye me Naomi, seeing the LORD hath testified against me, and the Almighty hath afflicted me?"

With today's passage, we once again encounter the significance of Hebrew names in the Old Testament. Naomi's name means literally "graciousness" or "sweetness." A careful reading of the entire book of Ruth identifies that it seems an appropriate name for this remarkable woman. Aside from the verses before us today, she manifests a consistent air of sweetness throughout. It might well be that these verses contain the overflow of emotions she must have been feeling as she and Ruth continually encountered the gossip we have already had occasion to notice. At any rate, she now reveals that her own heart is deeply burdened with the question that so often brings us all to the deepest despair: "Why?"

It was not enough that she had followed her husband, as his own faith wavered, to the unwelcome land of Moab and lost him and both her sons there. Returning home many years later, she has encountered the cruel innuendoes and suggestive gossip of those who could have been her truest comforters. Why, indeed, had the

Lord allowed such depth of sorrow to become her daily lot?

She suggests that everyone now call her Mara, which means "bitterness." She confesses before all that her heart is inclined now more toward bitterness than sweetness. She goes on to make it clear that she knows that such a terrible change of details in her life had to have been permitted by the God of Israel; she speaks of Him no less than four times in these two short verses. She imagines that He has some controversy with her, since He has "testified against" her and "afflicted her" (21). She knows little of the wonderful plans He has for her but will know soon enough. Weeping might endure for a night, but joy cometh in the morning. It will not be long before we find Naomi's faith once again taking the reins of her heart. And as we shall see, it will come as she turns her mind from her own struggles and seeks to reassure her daughter-in-law.

But, for a moment, let us return to that fact that even in her deepest distress, she is conscious of the fact that her God is still God. He is the Almighty, suggesting that all things are in His mighty hands and that the disposition of her own lot remains with Him as well. He is the Lord, the covenant-keeping God of Israel. His covenant with her people never had anything to do with their worthiness. Their own history is filled with examples of His grace and power overruling when their own rash sinfulness would seem to have disqualified them from His blessing at all. May it not be so for her, even if her husband's rash unbelief in a critical moment had brought them all to ruin and dishonor among their people?

And for us, is there no hope when we have also made rash decisions that would seem to set us outside His blessings? Are we Christians His people today because we in some way deserve such an exalted position among the sons of Adam? Or is it, in fact, all of grace? And if grace brought us into His favor to begin with, shall we always seek to find some way of having that favor restored when our own choices have brought us to Moab in a figurative sense?

Finally, it might be that there are some who will read these words who are enduring the ringing gossip of others for whatever reason. Do not let it make you bitter! Just around the next corner, there will be glorious joy yet again. We have much to read in this precious book.

RUTH 1:22

> So Naomi returned, and Ruth the Moabitess, her
> daughter in law, with her, which returned out of
> the country of Moab: and they came to Bethlehem
> in the beginning of barley harvest.

We have concluded that this first chapter of Ruth reveals that the redemptive love of God for His people is winnowing love. All throughout this chapter, that process of winnowing has been evident in the lives of Naomi and Ruth. If our reading stopped where we have come thus far, we would be left wondering what it had all been about. What could God possibly be doing in their lives that made all this difficulty meaningful? Is such winnowing really worth it?

But with today's verse, we get our first glimmering of hope. The first three words embody the faith that has sustained Naomi and begun to quicken her young Moabite daughter-in-law, Ruth. "So Naomi returned." Moab had never been her home. She had obediently followed her husband there years ago. It had been to her a land of death and despair. But now she has returned. And with her is Ruth, who, though a young woman, has had her share of distress. They have come all this way from Moab. Moab is to become, for both of them, a memory mixed with darkness and light, for if Naomi's husband had acted in faith during the famine those many years ago, Naomi and Ruth would never have met and the stage would not be now set for a far greater drama in both their lives than they had ever imagined possible.

Two women are coming into Bethlehem. One is an older woman who had gone out full and is coming home empty. The other is a young woman who had experienced nothing but deep emptiness in a nation God refers to as His wash pot. The emptiness of Naomi is magnified by the fact that she has no real prospects of once again being held in anything but the lowest esteem among her people now that all the men of her family have died. The uncertainty of Ruth is all the more pronounced because she is a Moabitess seeking acceptance among a people who have been commanded by their God to have no dealings with Moabites. Will things literally go from bad to worse for these two women? Or in their returning to Bethlehem, will there be a change for the better for them? The end of our verse for today holds the clue we need.

We are told that they came to Bethlehem "in the beginning of barley harvest." Harvest time in any agrarian culture is a time of great joy and expectation. There would be great celebration as the grain is brought in and everyone looked upon the fruit of their labors and God's blessing for many months. Another detail helps to heighten the hopes of these two dear women. Barley is commonly known as the grain of the poor. Wheat and other grains were often beyond the purchasing power of the poor, but barley was within their reach. After the barley harvest, the wheat harvest would come, as we shall see later in our contemplations. Additionally, among the Hebrew people, there was a curious aspect of their God-ordained manner of dealing with their harvests. They were commanded to leave the edges of their fields unharvested, allowing the poor to glean there freely.

So then we have some reason for hope and expectation for these two dear ladies returning at the time of the year when they did. They are coming to Bethlehem, the "house of bread." They are returning there in the time of barley harvest, the very grain that suggests God's care for the poor. There is immense celebration going on among Naomi's people. There will be gleanings available in the fields. And not long after the conclusion of the barley harvest will come the wheat harvest as well. All of this gives these outcast women much to rest their faith upon.

QUESTIONS FOR FURTHER CONSIDERATION ON RUTH 1:14–22

[1] Reread verses 15–17. Here we encounter Ruth beginning her journey to know the God of

Naomi. Just how far does a person have to go in terms of forsaking their previous life in order to go on with the Lord?

[2] How was it when you began your journey? Did you find yourself forsaking all else to know Him?

[3] Is there a sense in which He demands this of all of us all throughout our lives once we have been redeemed? To what extent?

[4] This week's passage closes with the two women coming into Bethlehem in the time of the barley harvest. Reflect on how the Lord has brought you to leave your own life behind but then led you into a far richer life as time went by. Is this His way? Does His winnowing always lead to His wooing?

[5] How might this first chapter of Ruth be helpful for you in providing encouragement for other saints who are facing difficult times?

WEEK THREE

RUTH 2:1–4

And Naomi had a kinsman of her husband's, a mighty man of wealth, of the family of Elimelech; and his name was Boaz. And Ruth the Moabitess said unto Naomi, "Let me now go to the field, and glean ears of corn after him in whose sight I shall find grace." And she said unto her, "Go, my daughter." ³And she went, and came, and gleaned in the field after the reapers: and her hap was to light on a part of the field belonging unto Boaz, who was of the kindred of Elimelech. ⁴And, behold, Boaz came from Bethlehem, and said unto the reapers, "The Lord be with you." And they answered him, "The Lord bless thee."

The passage of Scripture we have before us today is particularly rich in redemptive truth. If we look carefully, we will find numerous details that introduce us more fully to what the Lord is doing here. The first hint of precious redemptive truth is brought out in the very first sentence: "And Naomi had a kinsman of her husband's, a mighty man of wealth, of the family of Elimelech; and his name was Boaz." There are at least two important things this sentence places before us. First, if Elimelech, had this man as a kinsman years ago when the famine came, why didn't Elimelech turn for help to Boaz? If Boaz is a "mighty man of wealth," even after the famine, how much could he have helped Elimelech's family back then?

Surely this emphasizes the fact that we have been correct in thinking that his departure was an indication of his unbelief. Unbelief can take many forms, pride being one of the most prevalent. Perhaps Elimelech was too proud to ask for help from his kinsman. Now his widow will be forced to do so. How often does our pride move us to act in unbelief, causing us to miss what the Lord would do were we to humble ourselves and act in faith?

But this sentence places before us a second important detail. In it, we are introduced to a very important biblical concept, the concept of the kinsman-redeemer. When Moses wrote his inspired writings, he wrote of the responsibility of a near kinsman among God's people to take upon himself the care of the family of his deceased kinsman. It was another way they were to reflect the goodness and the glory of the Lord among them. The blessed reality we see here is that the Lord has a plan by which He intends to deeply enrich these two women who have come back to Bethlehem empty.

In verse two, we find Ruth speaking with her mother-in-law, humbling herself, willing to go out and gather the gleanings from the edges of someone's field. This was also commanded in the writings of the Lord through Moses. The poor among God's people were thus to be provided for in a marvelous manner. A rough equivalent in our culture today would be those opportunities for financially disadvantaged mothers to get milk and cheese or even food stamps through community programs. But in Ruth's day, there were no waiting rooms or long forms and interviews to be endured. She would simply find a field and walk along the outside edges of it, gleaning the grain that had been intentionally left there for such folks.

We are told that as Ruth went out to glean, "Her hap was to light on a part of the field belonging unto Boaz, who was of the kindred of Elimelech." The Lord uses this form of expression, I think, to show us how silly we are when we think that things just happen in a random way in our lives. There is nothing random about the redemptive purposes of God in Jesus Christ. And then, in our final verse for today, we actually meet Boaz for the first time. He has been mentioned, but now we encounter the man himself. And what sort of man is it that invokes the blessings of the Lord upon his laborers and is blessed in return? We shall soon see.

RUTH 2:5–7

> Then said Boaz unto his servant that was set over the reapers, "Whose damsel is this?" And the servant that was set over the reapers answered and said, "It is the Moabitish damsel that came back with Naomi out of the country of Moab": And she said, "I pray you, let me glean and gather after the reapers among the sheaves": so she came, and hath continued even from the morning until now, that she tarried a little in the house.

Our hearts might well begin to accelerate in their beating today as we read and contemplate our passage, for in it, we are privileged to be granted an inside look at the very first moments of connection between a wealthy man of Israel and a very poor girl from the despised land of Moab. How will it go? Will he even notice her at all? And if he does, will he, knowing that she is from Moab and adhering to every letter of the law of Moses, insist on having her cast out of his fields altogether?

Evidently Boaz does notice Ruth, for he asks his foreman who she is. He is told that she is the Moabitish girl that came back to Bethlehem with Naomi. Ruth had apparently not made any attempt at disguising her background, though she certainly would have known that anyone from Moab would be likely to receive less than optimal treatment. When Boaz heard that Ruth was associated with Naomi, he would have been very aware of the fact that Naomi was the widow of his own kinsman, Elimelech.

We are left to ponder what goes through the mind and the heart of Boaz as he receives this information. Here he has, in his own fields, a young woman from Moab, whose own life has been turned upside down. She is far from home and is herself also a widow. Did Boaz wonder what would have compelled Ruth to leave everything, casting in her lot with Naomi, when Naomi's own prospects were dim? Clearly, Boaz was a man who knew and deeply loved the God of his fathers. And he certainly grasped the enormity of Ruth's decision to depart from Moab with all its idolatry and paganism. And the stunning fact that this decision on her part had brought her to a position of embarrassment, having to glean ears of corn left for the poor among God's people, would speak volumes to Boaz about her genuine humility.

Boaz perhaps sits with his foreman as they talk and watches Ruth as she gleans nearby. He hears from his overseer that Ruth has been thus gleaning all day long, from early morning. Their discussion, as we shall see, covered more than the little bit we have before us in these few verses today. As Boaz listened to all that was being told him of this girl, did his heart burn within him? Was there any possibility that the same sovereign Lord who had brought this girl all the way from Moab was also at work to meet the deepest needs of this godly man's heart as well? We are reminded of the Lord providing a wife for Isaac from among those in a far country. But Boaz would nurture no misconceptions in his heart or mind. This young woman would have to entirely forsake the religion she had been nurtured in and turn to the God of Israel. This would take almost unimaginable courage and humility.

Boaz turns from his musings and his observation of Ruth nearby and hears his foreman telling him that this girl had politely and humbly asked for permission to glean there, and that she had been gleaning all day long. Once again, his heart skips a beat. She is a remarkable young woman. She has chosen to come to Bethlehem, knowing what it would mean. She has thrown in her lot with Naomi, apparently determined to do all she can to see to it that Naomi is cared for in her advancing years. Boaz can now hope and pray that the Lord has begun to turn her heart from the gods of her people unto the true and living God.

RUTH 2:8–12

Then said Boaz unto Ruth, "Hearest thou not, my daughter? Go not to glean in another field, neither go from hence, but abide here fast by my maidens: Let thine eyes be on the field that they do reap, and go thou after them: have I not charged the young men that they shall not touch thee? and when thou art athirst, go unto the vessels, and drink of that which the young men have drawn." Then she fell on her face, and bowed herself to the ground, and said unto him, "Why have I found grace in thine eyes, that thou shouldest take knowledge of me, seeing I am a stranger?" And Boaz answered and said unto her, "It hath fully been showed me, all that thou hast done unto thy mother in law since the death of thine husband: and how thou hast left thy father and thy mother, and the land of thy nativity, and art come unto a people which thou knewest not heretofore. The LORD recompense thy work, and a full reward be given thee of the LORD God of Israel, under whose wings thou art come to trust."

Today's passage brings us to the point in time in which Boaz and Ruth have their first conversation together. It was to have far-reaching results in the years ahead. Let us turn aside for a few minutes and see how the Lord was at work through this meeting.

In his first approach to Ruth, Boaz uses the utmost care to be entirely respectful, referring to her as "my daughter." This is not, as many assume, to be interpreted as an indication that Boaz was much older than Ruth. Instead, it very quickly identified that he was taking a position in which he was glad to, in a sense, become a provider for her. It would have helped Ruth understand from the beginning that Boaz regarded her with kindness and concern.

But Boaz goes on to strongly assure her that he truly meant his expression of concern when he implores her to give no thought to going into any other man's fields to do her gleaning in the days ahead. As we suggested earlier, the conversation between Boaz and his overseer had gone much farther than the earlier verses might have implied. He tells Ruth that he has spoken with his young men, and they are not to trouble her in any manner. He admonishes her to keep her eyes on whatever fields his own servant girls are gleaning in and follow along behind them, coming to the shelter area for food and drink when she needs them. He is essentially telling Ruth that he expects her to glean right along with his own servants. She cannot but be stunned by this display of kindness from a man she does not know and in a land in which Moabites have been historically despised.

She responds by prostrating herself before him and expressing her amazement at being treated with such grace and respect. Then Boaz identifies that he has learned from his foreman that she has behaved herself commendably in all that befell her in Moab, especially before and after the death of her husband. She has shown appropriate respect for her widowed mother-in-law and chosen to leave her own family to be of assistance to Naomi. More importantly, Boaz commends her for placing her trust in the LORD, God of Israel. It is precious when we first begin to trust Him and He responds by bringing us into contact with one of His choice servants who takes delight in our budding faith and encourages us by reflecting His grace toward us. This was the beginning of a wonderful relationship that furthered God's redemptive purpose for the world.

RUTH 2:13–14

Then she said, "Let me find favor in thy sight, my lord; for that thou hast comforted me, and for that thou hast spoken friendly unto thine handmaid, though I be not like unto one of thine handmaidens." And Boaz said unto her, "At mealtime come thou hither, and eat of the bread, and dip thy morsel in the vinegar." And she sat beside the reapers: and he reached her parched corn, and she did eat, and was sufficed, and left.

How precious are those first months when the reality of the Lord, in all His goodness and kindness toward us, woos us to Him. And as we proceed throughout this second chapter of Ruth, are we not seeing that His redemptive love in our lives is, indeed, *wooing* love? Today's passage carries on the revelation of God's wooing love as we see it reflected more and more in the demeanor of Boaz. We also see the stunned reaction of Ruth to the grace and kindness being displayed toward her.

In verse thirteen, Ruth is emboldened to ask of Boaz that she might find favor in his sight since he has already gone out of his way to comfort her and to speak to her as a dear friend, though she is clearly "not like unto one of [his] handmaidens." Ruth does not harbor any false hopes. She is deeply conscious of the prejudices that exist among the Israelites for her people. We must remember that she grew up in Moab, where prejudice toward those of Israel would have been as tangible and prevalent. She had not come back to Israel with Naomi blissfully unaware of the potential that existed for sore mistreatment at the hands of the people there. Yet, having "happed" to light in the field of this man, she is genuinely delighted to receive such good treatment instead. We can stand aside in the wings as we read the scriptural narrative and smile as the Lord begins His wonderful wooing process of this girl's heart through Boaz. Was there nothing of this same wooing as He found us where we were and, little by little, brought us to Himself as well?

Boaz responds to Ruth's open delight in his previous overtures by going farther. He tells her to come with his servant girls at mealtime and be fed right alongside them, as though she literally belonged under his roof and in his household. Ruth did come, and she did sit with the actual reapers of Boaz's household. Here she is, a girl from despised Moab, not sharing a scanty meal with the poor of the land but being fed right along with those servants whose blessed lot was to serve in the household of this godly man of staggering wealth. She could never, in all her wildest imaginings, have had any such expectation.

But there is even more. Not only is she eating and enjoying fellowship together with those girls who reaped the fields of Boaz, but she is receiving food directly from her new master's hand. We are told that he reached her parched corn, enough that she ate until she was satisfied. In our culture today, many would say it was like a fairy tale. To Ruth, it must have truly seemed like a miracle.

But wait, what is the most amazing miracle here? Is it the fact that a young girl, all of whose hopes had been dashed at the death of her husband, now finds herself being lovingly treated, even wooed, by a wealthy man in a country that had historically despised her people? Is it that this man is himself the son of a woman whose early lot in life had brought her to ill repute, or is it really greater than even these? Isn't it the blessed miracle of the powerful and relentless love of God, who will work through man's sin to bring the despised of the world to the center of His perfect will for their lives? It is well said that there simply is no one like Him.

RUTH 2:15-17

And when she was risen up to glean, Boaz commanded his young men, saying, "Let her glean even among the sheaves, and reproach her not: And let fall also some of the handfuls of purpose for her, and leave them, that she may glean them, and rebuke her not." So she gleaned in the field until even, and beat out that she had gleaned: and it was about an ephah of barley.

Ruth has sat down with the servant girls of the household of Boaz, even at a table presided over directly by the master himself. She has eaten until she is fully satisfied and has now risen up to return to her gleaning. But Boaz is being driven by something far bigger than even his own large heart. He speaks yet again to his young men, commanding them to allow Ruth to move in from the edges of the field and actually glean directly among the standing sheaves of grain. This is going a good bit farther than the revelation of the mind of God through the writings of Moses. In practical terms, Ruth is to be treated as though she were gleaning the field right along with the servants of Boaz.

But even that is not enough. Boaz finds himself outstripping his own generosity and benevolence. He commands his young men further that the girls who are gleaning for him, bringing in his own harvest, that from which he gained his own sustenance and good living, that they are to deliberately drop down much of the grain they are harvesting, leaving it to lie there for Ruth as she comes along. This is far more than good Christian charity. It is clear that this man Boaz is completely taken with this young Moabite girl.

We are never told the prehistory of Boaz personally. We do know that his mother was Rahab, that first fruits of the Lord's redemptive purposes when Israel came into the land under Joshua (Joshua 6:25). But as to Boaz himself, we know only what is put before us in this short book. Yet it seems clear that from the first moment he saw Ruth in his field he immediately began to act toward her as a man would toward a woman with whom he is smitten. We have already hinted at the blessed truth that the Lord who was working in the heart of Ruth to incline her to return to Naomi's people and come to Naomi's God, that this same God was working in the heart of Boaz, inclining his heart toward this girl in affection and grace. Does this surprise us?

Are we to believe as Ruth continued gleaning and the girls around and ahead of her continually seemed to be dropping more and more grain on the ground, that Ruth noticed nothing out of the ordinary? Surely she noticed as they would drop grain slightly farther into the field, away from the edges. Surely she would notice that she was moving farther into the field, picking it up. And are we to think that these servant girls did not notice their master behaving toward this Moabite girl differently than he had toward other poor folks previously?

Would they not have laughed among themselves and cast glances at this girl who had so singularly affected their master?

At the end of the day, Ruth gathered her gleanings and beat them to remove the heads of grain from the pieces of stalk. She had far more than she could have ever hoped for. She and Naomi would have by this time learned to live very frugally. It is one of the blessings of the poor. How cursed we are when we learn to live with an attitude of terrible waste. The blessings of our lives fail to seem like blessings when they are so easy to come by. This is merely the start of the barley harvest, and Ruth has already come home full. And this is really only the beginning of all that God has in store for her.

QUESTIONS FOR FURTHER CONSIDERATION ON RUTH 2:1–17

[1] Recalling these verses, what do you believe to be true about what folks might call "chance encounters?" How might this affect your prayer life?

[2] The Lord was using the details of everyday life to woo Ruth to Him. Can you suggest any ways in which this has been true in your life as well? How important are the little things in life to Him?

[3] Since Boaz was a wealthy man, yet devoted to the glory of God, how does this affect your attitude toward those whose wealth far outstrips your own? How can we pray effectively for those who are blessed with wealth?

[4] To what extent were Naomi and Ruth dependent upon the Lord for their daily sustenance? Is this true for you and your family as well?

[5] To what extent do you think American Christians are inclined to look to their own paychecks for sustenance, rather than to the Lord? How does what we have seen so far in Ruth affect your own thinking about our needs being met?

WEEK FOUR

RUTH 2:18

And she took it up, and went into the city: and her mother in law saw what she had gleaned: and she brought forth, and gave to her that she had reserved after she was sufficed.

Today's passage helps to clearly establish the relationship between Ruth and her mother-in-law, Naomi. And as we shall see, it establishes the breadth of the Lord's provision through the law of the kinsman-redeemer as it was to be applied in this particular instance.

Ruth had gleaned all day in the fields of Boaz. She had then done a preliminary winnowing of her grain and ended up with over an ephah of grain. This Hebrew measurement equates to slightly over a bushel of grain as we in America are accustomed to measure things. We must remember two things here. First, this is not just the unwinnowed grain but the grain having been fairly well winnowed by Ruth at the end of her day. Therefore, it would actually be slightly over a bushel of grain without the chaff. Second, this is what Ruth was able to harvest by herself in one day's work. This is a great deal more than, say, a bushel of maize (corn, as we know it) since one bushel of maize would have been easy to glean in a far shorter period of time.

So then, Ruth has come home to Naomi, bringing a bit more than a bushel of winnowed grain. As our passage reveals, Ruth shared her grain with Naomi and the two of them were clearly well pleased with the day's harvest. It is quite evident that Ruth had completely cast in her lot with her mother-in-law in that the two of them shared the fruits of Ruth's labors. In a culture such as that in America, it is not at all uncommon to find young or middle-aged people putting their elderly parents into homes where they can live out the remainder of their lives without being a bother to their children. Occasionally, one might encounter a person taking upon himself (herself) the care of a parent (or parents) as they advance in age. But it is becoming unusual. Rarer still is it to find a person taking upon himself (or herself) the care of a father-in-law or mother-in-law, especially if the spouse who had been the son or daughter to that elderly person has died. Clearly, the Lord is at work in Ruth's life. She has not only left her family and her gods, but she has committed herself to seeing to the care of her mother-in-law far from her own country and among a people who have every reason to shun her.

But these remarks bring us to another consideration. We have been delighted up to this point with the fact that it is the Lord, the God of Israel, who is at work in all that we have been seeing in this wonderful book. It was the Lord who sent the famine into the land among His own people. It was the Lord who worked through His relationship with Naomi to attract Ruth to Himself both before and after the deaths of their husbands. It was the Lord who was so personally precious to the man, Boaz, and who seemed to be inclining his heart toward this Moabite girl, Ruth. And long ago, in the days when this same Lord was working through the man Moses to write His words, He inspired him to write of the law of the kinsman-redeemer. As we shall see, this blessed law was intended to see to it that when a man died in Israel, his family was to be provided for and his name was not to be allowed to fail from among his brethren.

But today's passage begins to open our hearts to a deeper application of this law in the present situation. Ruth's relationship with Naomi was becoming so entwined that for the kinsman-redeemer to take upon himself the care of Naomi was also going to mean for him to take upon himself the care of Ruth (or vice versa). There is an enormity about the love of God.

RUTH 2:19–20

And her mother in law said unto her, "Where hast thou gleaned to day? and where wroughtest thou? blessed be he that did take knowledge of thee." And she showed her mother in law with whom she had wrought, and said, "The man's name with whom I wrought to day is Boaz." And Naomi said unto her daughter in law, "Blessed be he of the LORD, who hath not left off his kindness to the living and to the dead." And Naomi said unto her, "The man is near of kin unto us, one of our next kinsmen."

As Ruth brings in the fruits of her labors to Naomi, Naomi naturally asks her where she had been gleaning throughout the day. Naomi seems pleased with the fruitfulness of Ruth's harvesting since she pronounces a blessing upon the man who had evidently taken knowledge of her, permitting her to so fruitfully glean in his field. Ruth respectfully answers her mother-in-law, telling her that the man who had been so kind to her was a man by the name of Boaz. It is Naomi's response to this information with which we will concern ourselves today. There is great blessing awaiting us.

In the first portion of her response to Ruth's information, Naomi specifically says, "Blessed be he of the LORD, who hath not left off his kindness to the living and to the dead." Note that. She says that this man, Boaz, is to be blessed of the LORD in that he has shown kindness to both the living and the dead. What does Naomi mean by this odd saying? How does a man show kindness to the dead? More specifically, how has Boaz shown kindness to the dead? The only dead that have been in view all throughout the book are Elimelech, Mahlon, and Chilion. Therefore, we are certainly correct in presuming that these are the dead to whom Naomi refers in her benediction upon Boaz for his kindness.

For further help in understanding this peculiar manner of expression, we might consider the remaining portion of Naomi's response to Ruth. At the end of verse twenty, Naomi adds, "The man is near of kin unto us, one of our next kinsmen." This extra statement suggests why Naomi's own heart is so thrilled with Ruth's news that she had gleaned in the field of Boaz. He is not only a nice man or even a particularly kind man. It is far more than that. Naomi evidently knows her Bible (the writings of Moses) because she is beginning to get excited at the news that Ruth has happened to glean in the field of a man who happens to be near of kin to them, a man who, should he choose to do so, could fill the role of a kinsman-redeemer to them.

How our own hearts pound as we also come to see the providential hand of their God upon them. Going back in our minds to the scene in which Ruth departed from Naomi early in the same morning to go glean, we recall no urging from Naomi for Ruth to go to any certain man's fields to glean. Surely Naomi knew about Boaz, that he was a near kinsman, before Ruth went out. Yet, she clearly did not direct her to his fields. One wonders if Naomi was not merely leaving the disposition of all things in her life and in Ruth's life in the very capable hands of her Lord. Perhaps even as Ruth walked down the path, away from their meager abode, Naomi simply prayed that the Lord would guide her every footstep.

In any case, when Ruth told her that she had gleaned all day in the fields of Boaz, Naomi's heart must have leaped within her. The significance of today's passage lies in the fact that unless Naomi had been grounded in the Lord's written revelation, she would not have been excited about Ruth's news. One detail in an obscure passage leaped off the page to her.

RUTH 2:21

And Ruth the Moabitess said, "He said unto me also, 'Thou shalt keep fast by my young men, until they have ended all my harvest.'"

Our awe in the presence of God deepens because of how we see Him at work in the heart of Boaz, based upon the detail provided by Ruth in her report to her mother-in-law in today's passage. It is a short portion of Scripture, yet it is very precious indeed! May the Lord open our hearts and our eyes that we might worship as we read!

First of all, it is of the utmost importance that we not simply pay little attention to what we read in the first portion of our verse for today. It would be so easy to do. The phrase "Ruth the Moabitess" occurs five times in this book. The doctrine of verbal inspiration of Scripture teaches us that every word was literally given by the Lord Himself through His chosen writers. That being true, we realize that this phrase did not simply appear as some kind of personal style of the human writer of this book. The Lord wants us to remember every time we read this phrase this girl was from among the Moabites, people who had historically stood across the path, impeding God's redemptive purposes through His people, Israel.

But why would the Lord so continually remind us of this fact in this book? Is the Lord seeking to instill in us a form of prejudice? Does He want us to always be so conscious of the radical differences He puts between His own people and others? What can His purpose be in keeping this fact before us? There seem to be at least two key purposes the Lord has in reminding us that Ruth was a Moabitess.

First, He is reminding Israel and us today that there is a divinely ordained difference between His people and those who reject His redemptive purposes. Israel was never to forget this truth, and neither are we. The Moabites in their day had deliberately stood against the furtherance of God's purposes among His people. They had intentionally intermarried among the people

of Israel, acting on the advice of Balaam, who had coun-
seled Balak, the king of the Moabites, that to do so would
corrupt God's purposes among them. It is for this reason
that the Lord had forbidden Israel to have any further
dealings with the Moabites. All of this is placed before
us every time we encounter "Ruth the Moabitess."

Second, it would seem that the Lord is placing
something else, something very precious, before us each
time we encounter this phrase. As we have already seen
in our previous contemplations, there can be no doubt
that the Lord is sovereignly at work in the circumstances
recorded in this book to bring Ruth from her position
as a despised Moabite girl into the very line of the King
of kings. It should therefore amaze us each time we
encounter the phrase, "Ruth the Moabitess," because
it so clearly reminds us of the overruling grace of God.
The enemy had so powerfully worked through intermar-
riage between Moabite women and Hebrew men that
the Lord had found it necessary to forbid any dealings
between the two peoples. It is remarkable then that the
Lord Himself would work to bring one of those same
women into the lineage of His own Son. Yet, having
come this far through the Word of God, we are not at all
surprised to see the Lord working in precisely this manner. It is His way.

One other detail in today's verse bears mentioning.
Ruth says that Boaz had urged her to "keep fast by my
young men, until they have ended all my harvest." This
is such a wonderful encouragement! Not only has Ruth
been well treated on her first day of harvesting, but the
master of the fields in which she has labored has assured
her that he desires her to continually reap among his ser-

vants throughout the entire harvest process. God's grace is abounding grace.

RUTH 2:22

And Naomi said unto Ruth her daughter in law, "It is good, my daughter, that thou go out with his maidens, that they meet thee not in any other field."

The process of divine linking between Ruth and Boaz continues with today's verse. Naomi remains committed to the well being of her daughter-in-law and gives her simple advice. She tells her that it is wise and appropriate for her to follow the counsel of Boaz. Boaz had said for Ruth to keep fast by his young men, emphasizing the protective nature of their presence as she comes, day by day, to glean in the fields of Boaz. This is a man's perspective and entirely appropriate, particularly when Boaz wanted Ruth to feel secure and safe as she labored.

Yet, when Naomi mentions the same counsel from Boaz, she modifies the perspective, saying to Ruth that she is to "go out with his maidens." This small difference ought not to be overlooked in our hurried reading of God's Word. Naomi is speaking from the perspective of a woman and is actually emphasizing another matter to Ruth. Not only is Ruth to keep fast by the young men of Boaz, where she may be assured of her safety and protection, but she is to go out with his maidens, remaining among those who would be the objects of his personal solicitation and care. Boaz, it would seem, has the reputation of showing special concern and care for his female servants. But we are once more left to speculate about something very precious that is still rather below the surface at this point.

We have had the distinct impression up to this point that the Lord is at work in this entire process on both ends. That is, He has certainly been at work on Ruth's end, in Moab, to bring her heart to a favorable place of receiving His infinite grace on many levels. By the time she came to Israel with Naomi, she was open and ready for far more than she had even realized. But the Lord had been working on the other end as well. It is remarkable that this man, Boaz, who had to be one of the most eligible bachelors in Israel, was unmarried at this point. For whatever reason, Boaz was unwed and beginning already to manifest more than a cursory interest and concern about this Moabite girl. It seems likely that the Lord was working in his heart to draw him to Ruth so that the divine purpose of furthering the line of the Messiah might be fulfilled.

All of this is most instructive for us today as well. Why is it that we so often fail to realize the involvement of the Lord in these small, everyday relationships and events? Why do we relegate His earth-moving, redemptive involvement to high and staggering events in our thinking? He is at work in all of the small, everyday details, inclining our hearts one way or the other, developing relationships, working through needs and longings, in all these things accomplishing His own redemptive purposes.

Naomi gave an even more expressive framing of her concerns and desires for Ruth when she said, "That they meet thee not in any other field." She emphatically did not want the maidens of Boaz to encounter Ruth gleaning in another man's field. She felt strongly about what the Lord was doing in the heart of Boaz and wanted nothing to give ammunition to the enemy that could be used to suggest to Boaz that Ruth was in any way inclined to seek or accept help from another. Appearances are definitely not everything. In our day, we are inclined to lay more than appropriate emphasis upon them. Nevertheless, here is a situation in which appearances could have conveyed a wrong message. If Boaz only encounters Ruth in his own fields, he will be encouraged to realize that it is of the Lord that he draw closer to this Moabite girl. And while Naomi is certainly no matchmaker, she can see that the Lord seems to be linking Ruth and Boaz.

RUTH 2:23

So she kept fast by the maidens of Boaz to glean unto the end of barley harvest and of wheat harvest; and dwelt with her mother in law.

Today's passage brings us to the end of chapter two and places one further detail before us. We are told immediately that Ruth obeyed the counsel of Naomi and kept fast by the maidens of Boaz, gleaning only in his fields. We are left to ponder how many scenes such as we encountered earlier in this chapter, in which Boaz and Ruth conversed with one another, might have taken place.

We are not left to ponder how long this process continued since we are specifically told that Ruth gleaned alongside the maidens of Boaz throughout both the barley harvest and the wheat harvest. The best estimates of the duration of these two harvests suggest that it would have covered a period of about three months, the two harvests being associated with the feasts of Passover and Pentecost respectively. So then Ruth gleaned among the maidens of Boaz, coming under the direct protective care of his young men, for no less than three months. What a stark difference between her days in Moab and her early days in Israel! She went from being among the poorest in her own land, a widow with no prospects, to gleaning in the fields of one of the wealthiest men in Israel at his personal behest for three full months.

It should also be noticed that these two crops had their own particular markets. Barley was the cheaper of the two grains, being quite hearty as well as easier to harvest and was therefore sold more cheaply in the marketplace. Wheat, on the other hand, was less hearty and harder to harvest, the winnowing process often quite a bit more trying and demanding and was, therefore, more expensive when in the marketplace. Few among the poor could really hope to have wheat.

Yet Ruth was not only allowed but strongly encouraged, if not admonished, by Boaz to glean in both harvests. She took home for many weeks not only the grain of the poor but bushel after bushel of the grain of the well-to-do. This is certainly something that neither she nor Naomi could have anticipated. Not only would they now have sufficient barley for the fall and winter but far more. And the wheat would be like dessert. If Ruth was able to glean a bushel on her first day of barley harvest, we might even wonder where she and Naomi would have been able to store all the grain they harvested over both harvests.

All of this is remarkable merely on the everyday life level of things. But there is also the underlying reality that must be considered. Everything we have seen clearly suggests that both of these women who had come back to Bethlehem empty were no longer to find themselves empty. It is evident that they have already been taken under the sheltering arms of a wealthy kinsman, though not officially at this point. Furthermore, they seem to be the object of special attention of One far more wealthy and far more powerful still. Naomi, who, upon reentering among her own people, had said, "Call not thou me Naomi, but Mara," is most likely inclined to think otherwise now. That same God who had seemed to be against her now seems to be pouring out blessing far beyond anything she might have hoped for.

From these things we may take instruction. As we have seen, God is always at work in the minutiae of everyday life to bring about His wonderful redemptive purposes among us. It might be something as simple as providing for our health and wellbeing more than we thought He could or would or in drawing together two hearts to open the way for the display of His glory.

QUESTIONS FOR FURTHER CONSIDERATION ON RUTH 2:18-23

[1] In these verses we begin to encounter the concept of the near kinsman in Israel. How do you think would it affect American culture if we

followed God's plan for those whose spouses had died leaving them destitute?

[2] How do you feel about placing elderly parents into nursing facilities as a general rule? How do you think God feels about this practice that is so prevalent in American culture?

[3] Seeing Boaz beginning to minister to these two women at this point reminds us that the Lord was working on both ends of things, in Moab and in Bethlehem. How can we sustain the faith to believe that He is doing this in our own lives?

[4] How does this book of Ruth affect the way you think about finding a spouse? Is the cultural norm in America the same as what we have before us in Ruth? Did Ruth date numerous men before settling on Boaz? How much did she trust the Lord? How much do we?

WEEK FIVE

RUTH 3:1-2

Then Naomi her mother in law said unto her, "My daughter, shall I not seek rest for thee, that it may be well with thee? And now is not Boaz of our kindred, with whose maidens thou wast? Behold, he winnoweth barley to night in the threshingfloor."

With today's passage, we move from the earlier preparatory portion of this wonderful book into the very heart of all the redemptive will of God for this young woman, Ruth. Her mother-in-law, Naomi, now begins to speak more clearly to Ruth about the possibility of the Lord's intervention in their lives through a near kinsman, Boaz, the man in whose fields Ruth had been gleaning all throughout both the barley and the wheat harvests.

Naomi's first remark to Ruth, as it is recorded in this passage, is more important than it might appear to be upon the surface. She asks Ruth, "Shall I not seek rest for thee, that it may be well with thee?" Her question really embodies all her hopes for Ruth and, in a sense, for herself as well.

All throughout Scripture, there is a clear emphasis on the believer entering into rest. The Lord, Jesus

Christ Himself plainly invites all to come unto Him and, "Ye shall find rest unto your souls" (Matthew 11:28). In Hebrews 4:3, we are told that, "We which have believed do enter into rest." Rest is something the genuine believer expects, something he understands to be his (her) birthright in Christ. But how does this apply to Naomi and Ruth in this Old Testament setting?

As we have seen, both Naomi and Ruth have come through a very traumatic winnowing process as the Lord has worked to begin to bring them unto Himself and deepen their relationship with Him. Naomi has lost all the men folk in her family. Ruth had found it necessary to leave behind everything that had been important in her life. They had both returned to Bethlehem, one under the shadow of at least mild disgrace, the other as an outcast. They had found it necessary to throw in their lot with the poor of the land, gleaning at the edges of the fields for sustenance.

But, in chapter two, we have seen that a wooing process has begun, as Boaz has taken special personal notice of Ruth and required his servants to make special provisions for her all throughout the barley and wheat harvests. We have considered that, behind the scenes, there is an even greater wooing process going on. The same Lord who had manifested His great love for these women by winnowing them has now begun to woo them. It is the Lord who is drawing the two of them into something far bigger than they could have ever dreamed possible.

It is this wooing process that is before us in today's passage. But the focus in Naomi's remark is upon the ultimate goal of that process. It is, as we have seen, rest.

Naomi encourages Ruth's faith that the Lord is definitely involved in all that they have experienced since He has sovereignly brought them into contact with Boaz, a man who is a near kinsman to her former husband, Elimelech. She is suggesting that the Lord may very well be arranging things so that this man may take upon himself the role of the kinsman-redeemer, something the Lord made provision for in the sacred writings of Moses.

Perhaps the Lord is beginning a process that will result in both Naomi and Ruth genuinely coming into rest. It might be that, through this godly man, the Lord will more than meet their needs. Rather than being outcasts and the object of local gossip, they might find themselves being honored and respected. It might be that their long night of weeping and grieving is coming to an end. To this end, Naomi encourages Ruth to take certain appropriate steps, as we shall see.

RUTH 3:3–5

"Wash thyself therefore, and anoint thee, and put thy raiment upon thee, and get thee down to the floor: but make not thyself known unto the man, until he shall have done eating and drinking. And it shall be, when he lieth down, that thou shalt mark the place where he shall lie, and thou shalt go in, and uncover his feet, and lay thee down; and he will tell thee what thou shalt do." And she said unto her, "All that thou sayest unto me I will do."

This portion of Scripture is one of the most intimate and precious passages to be found anywhere in Scripture outside the Song of Solomon. It provides us with the inside look at a process of which we would otherwise have no knowledge. We can read the passages of Moses's writings that delineate the provision of the kinsman-redeemer and gain an outside grasp of the heartbeat of the Lord in making such a wonderful provision. But that does not give us anything like an understanding of just how such a thing would work out in relationships between real people. How would people feel about getting involved with such a process by which a man would literally raise up seed to a near kinsman? And how would it play out for a man to take possession of the property of another under such difficult conditions?

Note well the sweet submissiveness inherent in Naomi's instructions to Ruth. Ruth is to take all the steps in preparing herself as she would take were she to be appropriately wooing a man whose attentions she would hope to attract. And she is to go to the threshing floor where he would be working and celebrating with his servants in the final stages of the harvest process. But she is not to make her presence known unto him until later.

We must recall that Ruth has already been seen by Boaz day after day, gleaning in his fields all throughout the three months of barley and wheat harvest. We have every reason to believe that the attentiveness Boaz displayed for her wellbeing on her very first day of gleaning would have continued. His solicitude for her would now have been common knowledge among all his servants. But the portion of the harvest that Ruth would have had any part in was now over. She had her grain; months' worth of harvesting had provided both her and Naomi with more than they would probably need for the entire winter and well into the spring. The threshing going on in the threshing floor would really have nothing to do with these two ladies any further. So then, everything that Naomi is urging upon Ruth goes beyond the Lord's provision regarding their physical needs for food. As we shall see, this is the initial stage in what will have a far greater impact on their lives (as well as the lives of many others) as the Lord continues to fulfill His wonderful redemptive purposes for the whole world.

But first things first. If these events are to transpire, it is necessary that Ruth avail herself of what lies before her. She must humble herself yet further, placing herself in a position that plainly says to Boaz that she understands his overtures toward her in a very specific way. This she is to do without anyone else having knowledge of her actions. She is to wait until he has separated himself from the celebrating crowd and gone aside to take his rest. Once he has done that, she is to go to him, uncover his feet, and lay herself down at the foot end of his pallet. In doing so, she will be taking the most humbling position she could possibly take. And in doing so, she will also be relieving Boaz of any unnecessary pressures he might have been experiencing regarding his own personal feelings about Ruth. If he is to take the process of becoming a kinsman-redeemer forward, he needs to know that Ruth desires him to do so and that she will fully humble herself to whatever it will require of her.

RUTH 3:6-8

And she went down unto the floor, and did according to all that her mother in law bade her. And

> when Boaz had eaten and drunk, and his heart was
> merry, he went to lie down at the end of the heap of
> corn: and she came softly, and uncovered his feet,
> and laid her down. And it came to pass at mid-
> night, that the man was afraid, and turned himself:
> and, behold, a woman lay at his feet.

At the very end of the passage we considered yesterday, we found Ruth acquiescing to all that Naomi had placed before her regarding the next step in the process of Boaz being given the opportunity to become a kinsman-redeemer for these two women in Israel. From what we have seen up to this point, it seems that Boaz has given what might be thought of as "signals" that he would be interested in such a thing. But is it possible that Ruth and Naomi are simply reading into his actions something they have been so deeply longing for? Are they seeing things that aren't really there?

So, Naomi has instructed Ruth to take certain steps that would presumably open the way for Boaz to begin to "take the reins" in the kinsman-redeemer process. And, as we began to suggest earlier, we are granted a behind-the-scenes look at how this process would work out personally in the lives of real people. This is especially wonderful since Scripture does not reveal any of this in any other context. Apart from this inside look in the book of Ruth, we are left to view the kinsman-redeemer process from a basically theoretical perspective.

Ruth is being expected to deeply humble herself in order for both she and Naomi to ultimately come under the care and provision of Boaz as their near kinsman. She enters the threshing floor but does not make her presence known to Boaz. After Boaz is finished with the celebration for the evening, he moves away from the others, finding his way to the pallet that has been set up for him at the end of a large heap of the winnowed grain. We pause for a moment to delight with Boaz in the goodness of the Lord. Boaz has now come through two harvests: the barley harvest and the wheat harvest. He lays himself down to sleep in view of a huge heap of wheat as it has been gathered and stacked, ready for being transported to the marketplace. As he lies there, drifting toward sleep, his heart is overwhelmed with the Lord's faithfulness in his life. Even through the famine that so recently gripped his land, Boaz has been sustained, not losing everything but maintaining his crop output. He has much to be grateful for.

But just as he is drifting toward slumber, his attention is drawn to movement at his feet. He might have thought at first that some small animal had gotten into the threshing floor. But lifting himself up on his elbow, he looks only to see a girl laying herself down at his feet. While he is clearly aware that it is a person laying down and even covering herself with a portion of his blanket, he is at first unclear about who it is. It is at this point in the narrative that we again encounter the genuine godliness of this man. He could have developed any kind of relationship he might have desired to have with any one of his servant girls. Were he a vile man, he might have even sustained several such relationships. Immorality was no more alien to those in Israel than it has ever been among the fallen sons of Adam throughout human history. Boaz would not have far to look back in his own family history to encounter its ugly countenance. His own mother, Rahab, had at one time been a woman who sold herself for sustenance. Farther back, he would have heard of his forefather, Judah, and his illicit relationship with a young Hebrew girl that had been betrothed to his own son. What kind of a man is Boaz?

RUTH 3:9-10

And he said, "Who art thou?" And she answered, "I am Ruth thine handmaid: spread therefore thy skirt over thine handmaid; for thou art a near kinsman." And he said, "Blessed be thou of the LORD, my daughter: for thou hast showed more kindness in the latter end than at the beginning, inasmuch as thou followedst not young men, whether poor or rich."

Ruth has humbled herself about as far as she possibly can. It began as she made the choice to leave her own country, her own people, and her gods, casting in her lot with her mother-in-law, Naomi. It deepened as she came into a country and a culture that was steeped in abhorrence for her people. It continued as she took her place, dwelling among them along with an older Hebrew woman who would have also been looked at askance since the Lord had taken away all her men folk. Further still, Ruth had taken the public place of proclaiming herself to be destitute, having to depend upon the charity of others for her wellbeing and provision. She had gleaned in another man's fields for three months, she and her mother-in-law being sustained entirely by the gleanings she had gathered. Now the harvests are complete and Ruth has been asked to humble herself yet more deeply, laying herself down at the feet of Boaz, taking what had to be perhaps the lowest place in that culture. A very important moment has now come.

Boaz, perhaps being awakened by stirring at his feet while he slept, becomes aware that a girl has lain down at the foot of his pallet. He asks who it is that has done such an unusual thing. Already, Boaz has made it clear that he is a moral man, not interested in taking advantage of his position in life, though many lesser men have used just such social status to take liberties with young women in their employ. Having plainly asked who it is that has thus encroached upon his private sleeping space, Boaz is almost certainly delighted (based upon what we have seen in his previous attentiveness to Ruth) to hear the voice of the Moabite girl. He had just a short time ago drifted off to sleep with his heart full of praise for the faithfulness of the Lord in prospering his harvests so wonderfully. Now he awakes with the voice of this delightful girl he has come to care for very deeply lilting in his ears.

Ruth identifies herself, and we note clearly that she does *not* speak of herself as "Ruth, the Moabitess." This phrase occurs five times in this book, but Ruth does not use it here. She is at the very point of asking to be entirely disassociated with that background in her life. She asks Boaz to "spread his skirt" over her. This simply means that in placing herself beneath the very end of his bed covering, she is asking him, figuratively, to take upon himself her sustenance and care far beyond the current season of harvest. She specifically says to Boaz that he is a near kinsman. She is plainly telling him that she would delight if he, being a near kinsman to her deceased husband, will perform the part of a kinsman-redeemer for her and for Naomi as well.

With regard to Ruth, this would mean that Boaz would commit to raising up seed unto Mahlon (and Elimelech) so that their family name would not be lost in Israel. In other words, Boaz would commit to bringing Ruth to childbirth. Naomi would not have the same expectation, being much older. But her husband's name would be carried on through the seed of his son's former wife, Ruth. So, in performing the part of the kinsman-redeemer for Ruth, Boaz would being doing so for Naomi as well. Boaz's response at the end of our passage makes it very clear that he is delighted that she has asked him to take this responsibility! God is good!

RUTH 3:11–13

And now, my daughter, fear not; I will do to thee all that thou requirest: for all the city of my people doth know that thou art a virtuous woman. And now it is true that I am thy near kinsman: howbeit there is a kinsman nearer than I. Tarry this night, and it shall be in the morning, that if he will perform unto thee the part of a kinsman, well; let him do the kinsman's part: but if he will not do the part of a kinsman to thee, then will I do the part of a kinsman to thee, as the LORD liveth: lie down until the morning.

Once again we hear Boaz refer to Ruth as "my daughter." Together with his expression of delight that Ruth has not followed the younger men (verse ten), we surmise that Boaz was somewhat older than Ruth. Also, as we have previously mentioned, he uses this phrase as an expression of the utmost respect for her. Evidently, Boaz was not a married man and had no heir of his own. He is free to take upon himself the role of the kinsman-redeemer without entangling himself with any complications that would have been associated with his own family were he married.

He understands what Ruth is asking of him, as his response reveals. But his mode of response brings out an important detail. He says that he would delight in fulfilling Ruth's request, since "all the city of my people doth know that thou art a virtuous woman." We are left to presume that had she not been a virtuous woman (recall Proverbs 31:10ff regarding the scriptural identification of a virtuous woman), Boaz would have been free to set aside any expectation that he perform the role of the near kinsman unto her.

But Boaz is quite aware that there is a man who is actually nearer of kin to the family of Elimelech than he is. This man has the priority in accepting the responsibility and the ownership of any properties that would entail upon him from Elimelech's former holdings. Boaz wants very much to enter fully into this endeavor but cannot and will not overstep any boundaries or limitations that Scripture would necessitate. So he tells Ruth that he will speak with this other kinsman the next morning.

We must pause now to consider things as they have developed under the sovereign watch of the Lord. It is this far along in the narrative before we have had any mention of another kinsman nearer to Elimelech than Boaz. Is this a surprise to us? Are we now to panic, afraid that some other man, a veritable stranger, will now usurp the role that the Lord has been so assiduously preparing Boaz to play? It is of the utmost interest that we never learn the name of this nearer kinsman. Did the Lord know who this man was? Did the Lord know that there was another kinsman who would have the prerogative to entirely set aside the romance that the Lord had such a part in engendering in the first place?

One wonders if Boaz tossed fitfully the remainder of that night, fretful that now that Ruth had so plainly made her desires toward him known, another man who had had no part in the unfolding drama up to that point would step in and rend everything? And what about the tenderhearted Moabite girl? Was she now entirely satisfied that, no matter how things turned out in the morning, she would be taken care of?

Oh, we of little faith. Surely both Boaz and Ruth had been much in prayer for months now, as well as Naomi. Shall not the judge of all the earth do right? Will He draw the hearts of these two together only to leave them entirely estranged from henceforth? Even Boaz's remarks suggest simple faith, as he refers to his God as the LORD who liveth.

QUESTIONS FOR FURTHER CONSIDERATION ON RUTH 3:1–13

[1] In this chapter of Ruth we have seen that the Lord's love is unresting love. What impact does this fact have upon your own faith? What impact does it have on your patience with other saints?

[2] From your own consideration of these verses, mention any characteristics of Ruth's behavior that indicate she is resting in the Lord. How does this affect your commitment to enter into rest?

[3] There was much immorality in the Messianic line through the tribe of Judah, as we have seen. How do you account for God's choice of sinful men in the direct line of the Lord Jesus Christ? How does this affect your understanding of God's redemptive purposes in the world today?

[4] In Boaz's comments to Ruth in these verses he makes it very clear that everyone in Bethlehem had noticed that Ruth was a virtuous woman (verse 11). Is this manner of godliness something you would expect to see as a sinner is being wooed by the Lord? What should we think about those who say they are going to heaven when they die, but do not manifest this same godliness?

[5] Are you beginning to see the relationship between Boaz being a near-kinsman for Naomi and Ruth, and the Lord being a near-kinsman for all sinners everywhere? How does this affect your delight in being adopted into the family of God through Christ?

WEEK SIX

RUTH 3:14

And she lay at his feet until the morning: and she rose up before one could know another. And he said, "Let it not be known that a woman came into the floor."

With today's verse, we begin our consideration of the last portion of the third chapter of this wonderful book. As we continue, we are struck once again with the sense that the Lord who has been winnowing and wooing these women will not rest until He has brought them fully through into His rest. Naomi has clearly expressed early in this chapter that she intends to continue seeking rest for Ruth. This is a reflection of the Unresting God who has been at work for centuries among the fallen sons and daughters of Adam, seeking to bring them into rest.

Ruth has gleaned in the fields of Boaz all throughout both the barley and the wheat harvests. At the urging of Naomi, Ruth has now begun the formal stage of requesting that Boaz perform the role of the kinsman-redeemer unto her and indirectly unto Naomi as well. In a very real sense, this course of action reflects the only meaningful hope these two women have. Apart from this form of intervention, two things would happen.

First, they would have no hope of sustained provision for all their needs. Naomi was somewhat advanced in age, and Ruth was known to be from Moab. Women in that culture were not afforded the same kinds of opportunities for employment as women in advanced Western cultures. The culture of the Hebrew people at this early time still reflected, to a great extent, the patterns and social structure instituted by the Lord. Women did not work outside the home. There were few, if any, single-parent families through divorce. Therefore, both Naomi and Ruth were very dependent upon God's provision for them through the "law" of the kinsman-redeemer.

But secondly, unless some near kinsman took upon himself the role of a kinsman-redeemer for them, the branch of the family, through the tribe of Judah down through Elimelech, Naomi's husband, would terminate entirely. Elimelech and both his sons were deceased. That branch in the family tree would no longer continue. Among the Hebrew people, especially among those in the Messianic tribe of Judah, this would bring a certain amount of disgrace upon them. So then, we can see that Ruth's petition to Boaz to take upon himself this role was no small thing.

She has covered herself with the bottom end of his bedding and lay there all night in a position of utter submission. Yet again, we find this young woman gladly taking the lowest position. Clearly, the Lord has already done much in her heart, as we know all too well how rare such humility is among us. In today's Western cultures, a woman being expected to humble herself in this manner would not only be frowned upon but grounds for litigation on the basis of discrimination. Yet, Ruth gladly places herself in such a position. Her humility can only be understood in terms of her blooming consciousness of the mighty God of Naomi and of Boaz.

As she arises to depart in the very early hours of the dawn, Boaz cautions her to move away unbeknownst to others. It would have provided rumors for the local grist mill had others become aware of her having spent the night at his feet. What a blessing it is to encounter in this man someone who deeply desires to bring no reproach of any kind upon his Lord. His commitment to take upon himself the responsibility of the care and nurture of these two women was above reproach. Yet he was careful to "let not his good be evil spoken of." Everywhere we cast our eyes in this remarkable narrative we encounter God's handiwork in human hearts. May it be so among us as well.

RUTH 3:15

Also he said, "Bring the vail that thou hast upon thee, and hold it." And when she held it, he measured six measures of barley, and laid it on her: and she went into the city.

Today's verse provides us with a detail that in many ways might be considered unnecessary to the story being revealed to us here. Yet, it shows us more than meets the eye upon first consideration. May the Lord truly help us to receive the greatest benefit from it.

It is wonderful, first, to pause and reflect upon the fact of divinely inspired Scripture as a whole. What a remarkable treasure we have before us. Many of God's people have not been well trained in how to read their Bibles. As a result, they often overlook the preciousness of these seemingly insignificant details. One of the simplest and yet most important lessons we must learn about Bible reading and Bible study is that we are always to read and study for the sake of coming to know the Lord Himself. In His revelation to man, the Lord seems to delight in including many small details that help us to know Him better. All too often, we approach our reading of God's Word from the perspective of how it is supposed to show us how we ought to be living. When this is our primary perspective, we are inclined to miss those passages divinely intended to deepen in us a sense of worship.

Today's passage has the potential to have exactly this effect in our lives. Ruth has awakened from whatever sleep she was able to garner at the feet of Boaz in the threshing floor. He has spoken kindly to her yet again, encouraging her that he will gladly take upon himself the role of her kinsman-redeemer, provided that another man nearer of kin than he chooses not to do so. He has also admonished her to slip out from the threshing floor quietly so that her presence will have gone unnoticed by others. He is a remarkable man concerned for the glory of His God and longing to bring no reproach upon Him. He is about to send Ruth away with strong encouragement but pauses to express again his high regard for her and his intention to provide for her.

Even on her way out from the threshing floor, having obtained his assurances of his intention to see to it that she and Naomi shall be provided for throughout their natural lives, Ruth has reason to marvel yet again at the goodness of the Lord. Boaz will not allow her to go out empty handed. He arises and fills Ruth's veil with as much threshed grain as it will hold. She returns in the wee hours of this wonderful morning with both a present provision and a future promise. How full her heart must have been as she carefully chose her steps out from the threshing floor, being cautious so as not to awaken anyone. As she made her way home to Naomi, she must have been utterly stunned at the new consciousness arising within her mind and heart that this wonderful God is infinitely more than enough to meet her every need.

There has been a discernible deepening of her faith as she has moved through clear stages of divine wooing. She began by tentatively gleaning at the edges of the field of a man she did not know. Soon, she was eating in the shelters with Boaz's reapers. Then she was told to come right along behind them, moving entirely away from the edges of the fields and literally gleaning all through the fields. While gleaning behind his girls, Ruth was continually surprised to see them deliberately leave behind them grain they had reaped, lying on the ground, ready for her to pick up and add to what she was gleaning.

Now, Boaz has assured her that he intends to see to her needs from now on and he has sent her home full again. This all reflects God's commitment to bless her beyond her wildest dreams.

RUTH 3:16

And when she came to her mother in law, she said, "Who art thou, my daughter?" And she told her all that the man had done to her.

Ruth has left the threshing floor of Boaz and is walking home to the sparse accommodations she and Naomi call home. It is in the very early hours of the morning; and as Ruth walks along, laden with a good bit more grain, she has much to occupy her thoughts. The goodness of the Lord has surely overwhelmed her. She had no clear sense of His mercy and grace until she made the decision to leave Moab and migrate with Naomi to Bethlehem. Even having made such a life-changing commitment, she had no certainty, humanly speaking, of things working out in the best possible ways. She was, after all, coming into a culture that had historically had every reason to have unkind feelings toward her and her people.

But surely as she walked along, carrying the grain Boaz had heaped upon her, she must have been stunned at how things had been working out. Even having some small expectations of Naomi's God, Ruth must have been amazed at the staggering extent of His kindness toward her through Boaz. Perhaps her thoughts had gone all the way back to the days when she had first met Mahlon and Naomi. She might have pondered the utter desolation she must have felt as a young married woman, when her husband was taken from her in death. But then his father had died as well and soon his brother also passed away. Everything must have felt hopeless to her.

But now she is coming upon her dwelling place, and it is clearly quite dark still since Naomi had to ask her who she was as she drew near. Even Naomi's question would have had the potential of deepening Ruth's sense of wonder. "Who art thou, my daughter?" Who, indeed! Ruth, the Moabitess, the young woman who had entirely cast in her lot with this older woman and her people, and her God. Ruth, the woman in the prime of her life, far from home, utterly destitute, and placing all her hope in a God she was only beginning to know. Ruth, the young woman destined to come into the royal lineage of the greatest King the world could ever know.

But, just now, Ruth, the weary young woman with her heart in her throat at the prospect that the man Boaz could have made such promises to her. Ruth, standing before her mother-in-law, holding out her veil, it being laden with yet more grain, enough for weeks of nurture for the two of them. She must have felt that she was somehow standing on the shoreline of a vast sea, the surface of which was utterly hidden to her but for a short distance out from the shore. What would the light of this new day hold for her, for the two of them?

Now she has the blessed privilege of witnessing to Naomi the staggering goodness of the Lord in stirring the heart of Boaz to already desire to be their kinsman-redeemer. Often, the work of the Lord in our hearts deepens immeasurably just through the retelling of it to others.

Surely these two women had their very own personal prayer and praise meeting right there in their humble abode as they pondered again the incredible faithfulness of the God of Abraham, Isaac, and Jacob. Moab, with all its sorrows, began to recede in its power to bring despair and anguish to them. Looking back gave way to looking ahead in ever-deepening faith. Who could tell what the future might hold for those in personal fellowship with this remarkable God?

RUTH 3:17

And she said, "These six measures of barley gave he me; for he said to me, 'Go not empty unto thy mother in law.'"

Our own hearts are quite full as we continue our contemplations of the goodness of the Lord in His dealings with Ruth and Naomi. The two women are perhaps now sitting in their home, rejoicing in all that the Lord has already done for them. All around them would be the earmarks of His faithfulness. They would have grain, more than they could hope to use throughout the coming winter months. And Ruth has come in with more, something in the neighborhood of four and a half gallons more of beaten grain. How often we might be equally awed by His faithfulness if only we did not think ourselves the blessers instead of the blessed.

There is much implied in today's passage as well as what lies on the very surface. Notice that Ruth relates to Naomi words spoken by Boaz but not previously recorded by the Holy Spirit. She tells Naomi that Boaz specifically said unto her, "Go not empty to thy mother in law." This helps us in at least two important ways.

First, it reminds us that the historical narratives in Scripture do not record everything that was done nor everything that was said in a given instance. Had the Holy Spirit not mentioned this remark in passing, as it were, we would not have known Boaz had made such a comment to Ruth. How much more did he say in his conversation with Ruth that evening or early that morning that is not recorded in Scripture? The question might be interesting, but it brings up an important principle of Bible study and of presenting Bible truths to others. When we give the truth of the Bible to others, we ought not to speculate too much upon what the Bible does not specifically mention. Faith is built upon the reception in the heart of Truth from God. It is not deepened through speculation.

But second, it is important to acknowledge that the Lord does record all that we need in Scripture. There is nothing missing that we need. For example, there is the classic passage in John's gospel (21:35) where we are told, "And there are also many other things which Jesus did, the which, if they should be written every one, I suppose that even the world itself could not contain the books that should be written." Surely these things would have helped our faith. How can we get along without them? The truth is that were they necessary for the full revelation of redemptive truth, the Lord would have included them.

In closing our thoughts on today's passage, let us marvel all over again at the tenderness and goodness of the Lord, revealed through Boaz. Boaz is clearly not only concerned about Ruth but also cares deeply about Naomi. His gift of yet more grain, identified as being for Ruth's mother-in-law, speaks volumes about his message to her that he fully understands what they are asking of him and that he fully intends to take it upon himself to accomplish it for them.

RUTH 3:18

Then said she, "Sit still, my daughter, until thou know how the matter will fall: for the man will not be in rest, until he have finished the thing this day."

This wonderful scene, picturing the sweetness of the fellowship between Naomi and Ruth as the Lord is wooing and drawing them further into His redemptive plan, closes with today's verse. Naomi counsels Ruth to now sit still and wait upon the Lord, essentially, as the matter is now entirely out of their hands. Ruth has humbled herself deeply, asking that Boaz take upon himself the responsibility of the kinsman-redeemer not only for her but for Naomi as well. Boaz has promised that he will press the matter on the morrow, the day which is now beginning to dawn upon them. One way or the other, this day will begin the next chapter of their lives.

There are times in all our lives, as children of God, when all that is left to us is the waiting. Why is it that this one responsibility is often the hardest thing for us? Is it because it takes matters out of our hands? Is it because we are so much more comfortable thinking we are handling things? How foolish of us to cherish the silly notion that when we are actively involved, busily scurrying about doing one thing or the other, that these are the moments when our faith displays itself to good account. The opposite is often the case. When we are laid up, out of action as it were, set aside through incapacity or illness, or perhaps plain helplessness, these are often the times when our faith shines the brightest.

Some might argue that Naomi and Ruth only had to wait a very short time. The day of their deliverance had already dawned. Faith was no longer necessary as they knew that one way or another, their lot would be settled that very day. True, yet was this really all that they hoped for? Was there no longing in the heart of Ruth for the lot to fall a certain way? Was she only looking for provision, or was she daring to hope for deep, abiding love as well? What are we waiting for from Him? Is it mere provision of needs? Will we be satisfied simply to have such and such a financial need met or some forward step in our careers secured? How far has the "Christianity" of our day deteriorated when we may be content with having Him as the great Blesser in our lives?

It strikes any reader of this wonderful book of Ruth that this young woman was hoping for a great deal more than an unending supply of grain for the rest of her life. She was daring to hope that the true and living God would restore her heart, that the horrible loneliness and barrenness that had become the norm for her could be replaced with joy and delight. She probably wondered if she was imagining that Boaz could actually care for her, that all her previous hopes with her former husband might actually be fulfilled with Boaz. And she was second-guessing herself in her interpretation of all that her new Lord was leading her into. Was she expecting too much? Did she have any right to expect that He could be so merciful and kind to her? After all, wasn't she exactly the kind of woman that ought to know her place and have no expectations of God at all?

At this point in time, we are left to wonder if Ruth knew anything about the background of the man she was falling in love with. It is very unlikely that she and Boaz would have yet had such personal conversations as would open the way for him to share with her the remarkable story of his own mother, Rahab. Yet the God who delighted in redeeming and reconstructing Rahab could certainly delight in redeeming and recreating a young Moabite girl as well. And the wonderful thing about it all is that He is like that even when she is busy second-guessing herself and her expectations. He is the God of innumerable chances.

QUESTIONS FOR FURTHER CONSIDERATION ON RUTH 3:14–18

[1] Ruth has now lain at the feet of Boaz throughout the night, demonstrating her desire for him to take upon himself the responsibilities of a kinsman-redeemer. How does this relate to the Lord's admonition when He says, "Ye have not because ye ask not"?

[2] Since Boaz is viewed by most Bible scholars as a "type" of Christ, what do you think we are meant to learn from Boaz's determination to see to it that these two women are taken care of? How determined is God in these same matters in our lives?

[3] How do you think Naomi felt when she heard Ruth's report of the comment of Boaz when he said, "Go not empty to thy mother-in-law" (verse 17)? What are your greatest hopes as you continue to move toward older age?

WEEK SEVEN

RUTH 4:1–8

Then went Boaz up to the gate, and sat him down
there: and, behold, the kinsman of whom Boaz
spake came by; unto whom he said, "Ho, such a
one! turn aside, sit down here." And he turned
aside, and sat down. And he took ten men of the
elders of the city, and said, "Sit ye down here."
And they sat down. And he said unto the kinsman, "Naomi, that is come again out of the country of Moab, selleth a parcel of land, which was
our brother Elimelech's: And I thought to adver-
tise thee, saying, 'Buy it before the inhabitants,
and before the elders of my people.' If thou wilt
redeem it, redeem it: but if thou wilt not redeem
it, then tell me, that I may know: for there is none
to redeem it beside thee; and I am after thee." And
he said, "I will redeem it." Then said Boaz, "What
day thou buyest the field of the hand of Naomi,
thou must buy it also of Ruth the Moabitess, the
wife of the dead, to raise up the name of the dead
upon his inheritance." And the kinsman said, "I
cannot redeem it for myself, lest I mar mine own
inheritance: redeem thou my right to thyself; for
I cannot redeem it." Now this was the manner in
former time in Israel concerning redeeming and

concerning changing, for to confirm all things; a
man plucked off his shoe, and gave it to his neigh-
bor: and this was a testimony in Israel. Therefore
the kinsman said unto Boaz, "Buy it for thee." So
he drew off his shoe.

The morrow has now dawned and we follow Boaz as
he begins to make good his promise to Ruth the previous night. He had told her that on the morrow, the
business of her redemption by a near kinsman would be
settled. Rather than go about his own business and simply wait until his path crossed the path of the man who
was nearer of kin to Naomi, Boaz goes to the gates of the
town and sits down there, knowing that the man would
pass that way as he took care of his day's toil. When the
man passed nearby, Boaz called unto him, asking him
to sit with Boaz and ten of the town's elders so that the
matter might be settled.

As they began their discussion of the matter at hand,
Boaz clarified the issue for everyone. The land that had
belonged to Naomi's husband, Elimelech, needed to
be redeemed, according to the law of Moses, so that it
would not pass from the tribal ownership of the tribe of
Judah. The opportunity to redeem the land defaulted to
the man who was nearest of kin to Elimelech. Boaz pres-
ents all of this quite clearly to the small assembly and
then asks the man if he will or will not redeem the land,
expressing his own personal interest in doing so should
the other decide against doing so. The man responds
that he will certainly redeem the land, buying it from
Naomi.

The business transaction seems complete until Boaz
also identifies that in redeeming the land the redeemer

would be responsible for also marrying Ruth and raising up seed unto the name of her deceased husband. This is the critical moment for both Boaz and Ruth, for if this other man can marry Ruth and is willing to do so, there can be no union between these two who have come to delight in each other.

But since the redemption of the land is entirely linked to the redemption of Ruth's deceased husband's good name in Israel, the kinsman cannot do it. Thus, Boaz was free to redeem both the land and to marry Ruth. Ruth's first son would bear his deceased father's name and would carry on the line through his family. The other children born to Boaz and Ruth would carry on the line of Boaz directly. All that remained was the sealing of the transaction by the custom of the putting off of the shoe, which they did. The consummation of all the redemptive will of God for Ruth is very near at hand now.

RUTH 4:9–12

And Boaz said unto the elders, and unto all the people, "Ye are witnesses this day, that I have bought all that was Elimelech's, and all that was Chilion's and Mahlon's, of the hand of Naomi. Moreover Ruth the Moabitess, the wife of Mahlon, have I purchased to be my wife, to raise up the name of the dead upon his inheritance, that the name of the dead be not cut off from among his brethren, and from the gate of his place: ye are witnesses this day." And all the people that were in the gate, and the elders, said, "We are witnesses. The LORD make the woman that is come into thine house like Rachel and like Leah, which two did build the

> house of Israel: and do thou worthily in Ephratah,
> and be famous in Bethlehem: And let thy house be
> like the house of Pharez, whom Tamar bare unto
> Judah, of the seed which the LORD shall give thee
> of this young woman."

Today's passage records the official establishment in Bethlehem of the right of Boaz to act as the kinsman-redeemer for both Ruth and Naomi by acquiring the land that had belonged to Elimelech, Mahlon, and Chilion and by marrying Ruth and raising up seed unto Mahlon. The ten elders that had witnessed the transaction, together with whatever people that had also been nearby and had also seen it, gave clear public testimony that all had been done decently and in order, according to the law of Moses.

We are left to ponder if Naomi and Ruth had perhaps drawn near while the transaction had been completed and if they had not held one another and wept for joy. The goodness of the Lord truly is beyond finding out. He had not only brought them back to the house of bread (Bethlehem) in the time of harvest but He had brought them into the protective care and wonderful nurture of a godly man under whose wings they may take full refuge. The terrible grief of having their branch of the family of the tribe of Judah terminated with the death of all the men in their family was now set aside. Boaz fully intends to raise up a son through Ruth who will carry on his father's and his grandfather's name in Israel. As we shall soon see, the Lord goes far beyond even this great restoration, granting to these two women the blessed privilege of being in the very branch of the tribe of Judah out of whom shall arise the One whose coming was the very fabric of all their hopes, and the hopes of a weary world as well!

But we must pause for a few moments to consider the preciousness of the faith of those who delighted in their blessedness from the Lord that day. Their remarks show plainly that their faith was alive and quite vigorous, even though these events transpired during the days when the judges ruled and faith was seemingly a rare commodity.

They express their prayers for Boaz and Ruth (and Naomi) that the Lord would bless them as He had blessed previous generations of their people through the fruitfulness of the wombs of Leah and Rachel, "which two did build the house of Israel." This reflects their faith in the Lord's promises to fulfill His worldwide redemptive purposes through these earlier women. But they go on still farther by saying also, "And let thy house be like the house of Pharez, whom Tamar bare unto Judah." There cannot be any doubt of their faith. They are expecting that through this union between Boaz and Ruth the Lord will fulfill His promise regarding the Redeemer arising from the tribe of Judah. May the Lord continue to raise up in our own day a believing remnant like this! How inclined we are to allow the measure of our faith to be determined by today's newspapers. Yet, He is busily continuing His blessed purposes right in our ordinary days.

RUTH 4:13–17

So Boaz took Ruth, and she was his wife: and when he went in unto her, the LORD gave her conception, and she bare a son. And the women said unto Naomi, "Blessed be the LORD, which hath not left thee this day without a kinsman, that his name may be famous in Israel. And he shall be unto thee a restorer of thy life, and a nourisher of thine old age: for thy daughter in law, which loveth thee, which is better to thee than seven sons, hath born him." And Naomi took the child, and laid it in her bosom, and became nurse unto it. And the women her neighbors gave it a name, saying, "There is a son born to Naomi; and they called his name Obed: he is the father of Jesse, the father of David."

This thirteenth verse is precious almost beyond expression. It makes a very simple and very common statement that could apply to countless unions throughout the history of mankind. Yet, in this specific case, it carries more than the simple statement can possibly convey. From our previous study of the record of the lives of these two persons, we bring a great deal with us into the statement before us.

Indeed, were it not for clear, divine intervention through the writings of another man (Moses) some hundreds of years before regarding the institution of the law of the kinsman-redeemer, there would be no such union taking place at all. Even further, however, were it not that this man, Boaz, truly grasped the staggering wonder of his God's infinite grace and himself interpreted the sacred writings given by the Lord in light of His infinite grace, this union certainly would have never taken place. Boaz's people had been divinely told to have no dealings with the Moabites of any kind. Yet Boaz knew, had personal reasons for knowing, that this prohibition could not mean an absolute rejection of unworthy Moabites. His own family radiated the grace of this same God toward unworthy women from among other peoples. We shall see more of this later.

We recall the history of this girl. She was, in fact, a woman from among the despised Moabites. She had no blood claim upon this man or his family. She had no reasonable expectation of kindness and mercy from them. Yet, having been encouraged by her mother-in-law to apply to Boaz for his grace in performing the part of a near kinsman unto her even though she had none of the blood of Israel in her veins, she has cast herself entirely upon the mercy of the Lord through Boaz. Boaz has beautifully reflected the kindness and mercy of His God unto her, and they are wed. Ruth is certain to be beside herself with unexpected joy and hope. Her future has brightened immensely now through the goodness of her new God, the God that had formerly been known only unto her as the God of Naomi.

The birth of the first male child of this union completes the contract of the kinsman-redeemer. It is for this reason that the child is viewed by those surrounding them at his birth as being the son of Naomi. The child will carry on the line of Naomi's deceased son, Mahlon, the former husband of Ruth. It is of the utmost importance that we not overlook their clear testimony of the faithfulness of the God who had miraculously brought all these things to pass. The same God who, some months previously Naomi had thought was against her in some way, was now clearly blessing her beyond her farthest imaginations. He delights in being such a God always unto those who put their trust in Him.

RUTH 4:18-20

Now these are the generations of Pharez: Pharez begat Hezron, And Hezron begat Ram, and Ram begat Amminadab, And Amminadab begat Nahshon, and Nahshon begat Salmon.

The book of Ruth is coming to its remarkable conclusion. It is short on words but not at all short on substance. We have seen that the Lord works through His redemptive love to bring every believing child of God into the center of His perfect will for him (or her). That divine love is seen to be winnowing love throughout the first chapter of this precious book. The revelation of His love deepens in chapter two, as we have seen it to be wooing love as well. The third chapter furthered our understanding of God's remarkable redemptive love, revealing it to be unresting love. He never rests in fulfilling His wonderful loving purposes in the life of every believer. Finally, in this stunning fourth chapter, we see that His love is unchanging. The remaining verses present this truth unmistakably.

Today's passage carries us back to a much earlier time in the history of Boaz and Naomi's people. We are shown the staggering love of this same God as He worked out His redemptive plan through deeply marred and clearly unworthy men. Pharez is the first we encounter in the abbreviated genealogy given to us here. Pharez was the illegitimate son born to Judah and a woman he thought to be a harlot but who turned out to be Tamar, a young woman unto whom he had promised his youngest son in marriage. Let us examine this peculiar incident further.

Here we have Judah, one of the twelve men who, as the sons of Jacob (whose name became Israel), stood at the head of the twelve tribes that sprang from the great patriarch. There is more, far more, for this man, Judah, not only stood at the head of one of the tribes of Israel but at the head of *the* tribe of Israel. It had been prophesied clearly that the promised seed of the woman, the God-ordained Redeemer Himself, would arise from this tribe.

Two things strike us in knowing this. First, how would it be possible for the Lord to select such a man as Judah, knowing ahead of time that Judah would commit such wickedness in an illicit relationship with Tamar? Furthermore, why would the Lord choose to carry the line of the coming Messiah directly through the offspring of that illicit union?

Second, if Judah had any intimation of his own tribe's destiny, how could he have engaged in such illicit behavior at all? Surely good men will walk circumspectly when cognizant of a high calling.

In both of these instances, the one thing that stands out is the character of the grace and mercy of God. Even in the lives of good men, men who know Him, there will be flaws, sins that beset them. What other kind of men does this merciful God have available to Him for the furtherance of His redemptive purposes? Only one Son of Eve has ever lived apart from the ravages of sin within His heart. If we are taught anything by these few verses before us we are taught the exceeding power of the grace and mercy of the God of Abraham. His redemptive purposes do not rise and fall with all the vicissitudes of the fallen sons of Adam.

Judah will enter into grievous sin with a young woman intended to be his daughter-in-law. Still, God's redemptive purposes flow through his life and family. Moab will be born of an illicit relationship between Lot and one of his own daughters and will head a people who stand against God as He works out His redemptive purposes through His people Israel. Yet a Moabite girl will be brought directly into the lineage of the tribe of Judah, from whom shall arise the King of kings. There is no plumbing these depths. It is left to us only to stand in awe of this God and His infinite grace. We do well to avail ourselves of it as well, as it is extended to all, however vile and unworthy we are.

RUTH 4:21–22

And Salmon begat Boaz, and Boaz begat Obed,
And Obed begat Jesse, and Jesse begat David.

Hallelujah! The Lord God omnipotent reigneth. So says the writer of the book of Revelation; and well he may, as his book stands at the close of an entire canon of sacred Scripture in which we continually behold Him reigning as He brings about His wonderful redemptive purposes (Revelation 19:6).

Today's passage, though brief, is rich in this same wonder and awe. We have already contemplated the wonder of redeeming grace as it is displayed in the early portion of the genealogy carried farther in today's verses. Now we encounter a statement about the birth of Boaz, the man called upon by the Lord to perform the role of kinsman-redeemer for Ruth, the Moabitess. We are told that Salmon begat Boaz. But of whom did he thus beget this son? It was of Rahab. This woman strode into this family history from a most unexpected background. Early in the sacred history recorded by Joshua we find Rahab, a Canaanite harlot, hiding the spies sent into Jericho by Joshua. Later, when the city was destroyed by the Lord, Rahab and her family (her father, perhaps her mother, and her siblings) were spared. Her history among God's people continues here. She evidently became quite a godly woman, as her son, Boaz, is clearly one of the godliest men encountered in the Old Testament.

And now Boaz, her son, has married a Moabite girl (Ruth) by whom he begets Obed. This child shall fulfill the requirement for Boaz in raising up seed unto Mahlon, Ruth's deceased former husband. But the blessing is only beginning. Not only does the name of Elimelech live on through the seed of his son's wife, but the Lord chooses to allow this very seed to be the one through whom the promised Messiah will arise. Elimelech manifested some measure of unbelief in leaving Bethlehem when the famine came many years prior to the birth of Obed. And unequivocally, he manifested disobedience to God's command through Moses to have no dealings with Moabites. Yet, when it is time for the line of the Messiah to continue through a branch of the tribe of Judah, it is through this very man's lineage that He will come.

We are specifically told that Obed later begets Jesse and that Jesse becomes the father of David, the great king of Israel. God tells David, the grandson of Obed and the biological great-grandson of the union between Boaz and Ruth, that his greater Son will sit on His throne forever. Thus, we see that a despised Moabite girl who married into the family of an errant Israelite eventually becomes the biological great-grandmother of David and is in the very human lineage of the Son of God.

How shall we relate to these things? What are they to mean to us today? Is it not that this same God has these same redemptive purposes for His children today? Are we to despair because of the winding paths our lives and our families follow? We are all born under sin. At our best, we are redeemed sinners. We have no worthiness in ourselves to commend us to Him. Yet He chooses to use us in the fulfillment of His wonderful worldwide redemptive purposes. Let us therefore trust Him completely, even in our darkest hours. He is deeply glorified because it is all of grace.

QUESTIONS FOR FURTHER CONSIDERATION ON RUTH 4:1–22

[1] In this chapter the thrust of this blessed book is brought out in the open. All that God has done in the lives of Naomi, Boaz, and Ruth is linked fully to God's eternal worldwide redemptive purposes in Christ, the Great Kinsman-Redeemer of all mankind. Take a few moments to write down your own sense of God's redemptive purposes for your life.

[2] This chapter goes far back into Hebrew history, tracing the lineage of this family in Bethlehem. What does it mean to you that God's redemptive purposes connect you with all of human history?

[3] Spend some time writing out how this wonderful book of Ruth has affected you.

   a. What has the Lord done in your life in manifesting His winnowing love?

   b. Think about all the precious ways that the Lord has worked, wooing you unto Himself. Are you committed to this same love becoming more and more a leading characteristic of you life?

   c. Make it a goal that you will never forget God's infinite patience in dealing with His children, as He refuses to rest until we are perfected in Christ. How can you help other saints to enter into His rest?

   d. God's love is unchanging love. Our love changes for many different reasons. How can your life more adequately reflect the unchanging love of God?

[4] Finally, as we conclude our contemplations of Ruth, ask yourself this question: Is it clear from my manner of life that I have rejected the idea that men are to do "that which is right in their own eyes," and have chosen instead to walk in humble faith with the Lord, entering into His redemptive purposes for me?